guitar

THIS IS A CARLTON BOOK

Published by Carlton Books Limited 2003
20 Mortimer Street
London W1T 3JW

A CIP catalogue for this book is available from the British Library.

ISBN 1 84222 581 2

Editorial Manager: Penny Simpson
Art Editor: Adam Wright
Design: DW Design
Jacket design: Alison Tutton
Picture research: Stephen Behan
Production: Janette Burgin

Printed and bound in Dubai

guitar

a celebration of the
world's finest guitars. Terry Burrows

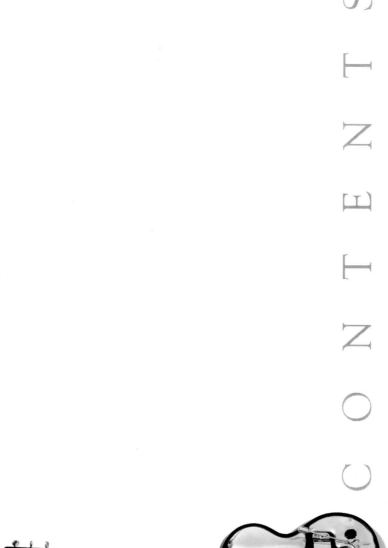

C O N T E N T S

G U I

INTROD

The guitar has existed in a recognisable form for the past four hundred years. However, it is only over the last half century that the guitar – and in particular the electric guitar – has become the dominant driving force in modern music. Indeed, it's hard to imagine what much of the last fifty years of rock, pop, country, blues and jazz music would have sounded like without it. Yet, although the guitar is in some ways a modern phenomenon, the instrument has a history that can be traced back well over four thousand years.

The origins of the guitar are shrouded in mystery. Its oldest surviving ancestors date from the fourteenth century, but how they reached that stage of evolution we can only guess. Certainly we know that stringed instruments designed to be played either by strumming or plucking existed many thousands of years ago. The earliest "evidence" we have is in Babylonian clay reliefs discovered in Central Asia. Carvings dating from around four thousand years ago clearly depict groups of musicians playing instruments that share a number of features with the instrument we know as the guitar – fingerboard, frets, the use of more than two strings, and what seems to be a resonating body. We can perhaps guess that the volatile cultural and political landscape of the region – not to mention the movements of the early merchants and traders – are likely to have spread the use and popularity of such instruments.

One ancestor of the guitar, a stringed instrument called the ud, found its way into Europe via the south of Spain, following the Moorish conquest in the eighth century. Evolving locally over the centuries that followed, the instrument gradually spread throughout Central and Northern Europe, giving rise to such offspring as the lute and gittern.

Appearing at the end of the fifteenth century, the earliest "true" guitars were actually closer in size to the much smaller lute. These instruments were notably different from their modern forebears. Rather than being tuned individually to different notes, strings were grouped together in pairs, or "courses"; each course was tuned to the same note. More dramatically, the fingerboard did not have frets fixed permanently in place, they were instead made from lengths of gut that the musician wrapped around the neck. The number and position of these frets depended on the "mode" of the music being played. This meant that before performing, the sixteenth-century guitarist not only had had to ensure that each pair of strings was in tune, but that the frets were positioned for correct intonation.

From the middle of the eighteenth century, the guitar

began a period of slow transition. The four- and five-course guitars of previous centuries gave way to six-course instruments. Gradually, courses were replaced by single strings and the modern E-A-D-G-B-E tuning system was adopted. Thankfully, the frets were finally fixed into the fingerboard. However, this same period also saw the guitar fall from fashion as the piano gained popularity.

The nineteenth century was a revolutionary period for the guitar. In Spain, the work of Antonio de Torres Jurado (1817–92) turned the guitar into a serious and credible instrument. Torres experimented with the construction and dimensions and created a template for the classical instrument that exists to this day.

At this time, however, the guitar rarely graced the great concert halls of Europe. It was largely the efforts the self-taught Spanish virtuoso Andres Segovia that the profile and respectability of the guitar escalated during the first half of the twentieth century. Through his influence, some of the finest composers of the past century – Villa-Lobos, Castelnuovo-Tedesco, and Rodrigo – have created seminal works for the guitar.

During the nineteenth century, other radical moves were taking place across the Atlantic where Christian Frederick Martin and Orville Gibson spearheaded the great American guitar tradition. Martin had learned his

craft in Vienna, apprenticed to the great luthier Johann Stauffer. In 1833 he emigrated to the United States, setting up a business in New York City. To this day, the Martin company is famed for the quality of its flat-top acoustic guitars.

During the 1880s, Orville Gibson produced a new breed of guitar that used construction techniques more commonly associated with violins. His instrument designs favoured a curved top rather than the traditional flat-top. By the time of his death in 1918, Gibson guitars enjoyed a reputation second only to Martin, and over the years that followed Gibson was to have a significant impact on the future of the guitar.

By the 1920s, the guitar's future was under threat as jazz (and to a lesser extent) country and folk dance bands became increasingly popular. The guitar's naturally low volume, when compared to horns and drums, meant that at best it could only be used to provide rhythmic backing. Indeed, until louder acoustic guitars were developed, the percussive sounds of the banjo was more commonly heard.

The ultimate answer to this problem came with the development of the amplified guitar. Although Gibson's Lloyd Loar had developed a magnetic pickup in 1924, the company failed to see its potential, leaving others to make the running. During this period, Hawaiian music became fashionable, and in 1931, Rickenbacker produced the cast-aluminium "Frying Pan" lap steel. Although it only barely qualifies as a guitar, it was the first commercially produced electric stringed instrument. A few years later, the company applied the same magnetic pickup system to an arch-top acoustic guitar, creating the "Electro Spanish" series.

The first electrics were viewed with suspicion by musicians. This changed in 1935 when Gibson launched the ES-150 model. In the hands of bebop jazz pioneer Charlie Christian, the electric guitar was introduced as a serious musical proposition.

Fitting pickups to an acoustic guitar may have started a musical revolution, but it also raised a serious new issue: "feedback". If the volume from the loudspeakers became too loud, the body of the guitar would vibrate, creating an unpleasant howling noise. A solution to this problem was to increase the body mass of the instrument so that it could not vibrate so easily. Thus, during the 1940s, the first solid-body electric guitars were developed.

Although nobody can claim with any certainty to have "invented" the solid-body guitar (although some have tried), it was Leo Fender who first put it on the production line. In 1950, the Californian radio repair-

shop owner created the Fender Broadcaster – the first mass-produced solid-body electric guitar.

The success of the Broadcaster (renamed the Telecaster shortly after) led Gibson to produce the "Les Paul", developed with the guitarist of the same name, who had been one of the earliest figures to experiment with the idea. Two years after the appearance of the Gibson Les Paul, Fender came up with the legendary Stratocaster, without doubt the most famous electric guitar of all. Indeed, the "Strat" now enjoys such iconic status as a design classic that even its silhouette would be recognizable to many non-guitarists.

By the end of the end of the 1950s there were many other manufacturers of fine electric guitars – Gretsch, Rickenbacker, Epiphone to name but a few. However, one thing was clear: whilst the guitar was a European instrument, the electric guitar was an American phenomenon. Trade sanctions in place at the time made it difficult and very expensive to acquire US-built instruments outside America. So, European and Japanese manufacturers rose to the challenge of providing their own instruments. With a few notable exceptions, most non-American electric guitars built before the mid-1970s were shameless rip-offs of classic American designs. Poor-sounding and difficult to play, they were nonetheless good enough for most fledgling guitarist of the 1960s and 1970s to learn their chops.

From the mid-1970s, the situation began to change. Japanese companies like Ibanez and Yamaha started to produce fine original instruments of their own. Others such as Tokai had refined their copies to such a degree that they came close to matching the quality of the originals, which were widely felt to have gone into decline during that decade.

As a result, the major players launched multi-tiered production systems in which "cheap" alternatives of their own classic designs were built in territories like Japan, Korea, and Mexico. This was a popular move allowing novices, or those with little money, to own genuine well-made Fender and Gibson guitars, while top-of-the-range US-built originals retained their own market (and correspondingly high prices).

It could be argued that in the years following the invention of the solid-body electric guitar there have been surprisingly few radical changes. Manufacturers have experimented with new shapes and materials. Attempts have also been made to integrate other technology, such as organs and synthesisers, but these hybrid instruments never achieved widespread popularity.

Perhaps this explains why, fifty years after their first appearance, the Fender Telecaster, the Gibson Les Paul, and the Fender Stratocaster remain the Holy Trinity of electric guitars. In fact it's hard to think of a single guitarist of any note who has not at some stage owned or used one or more of these hallowed instruments.

Intrinsically linked with innovations to improve sound quality, affordability and playability has been the quest by luthiers and manufacturers to make their designs stand out from the crowd, either though fine craftsmanship, innovative decoration or novelty design. Although the basic instrument may have changed little in principle, guitar design has always moved with the prevailing fashions of the day. From a visual perspective, the Rizzio Guitar of the late seventeenth century is, in its own way, every bit as "of its time" as the headless Steinberger of the 1980s, or Parker Fly of the 1990s.

Focusing on the creativity and craftsmanship behind each selected model, this unique book looks at the extraordinary diversity across acoustic and electric guitars, and celebrates the most dazzling among them, from the classic solid-body electric Gibson Flying V and novelty solid-body electric Framus "Super Yob" specially built for Slade's Dave Hill, Prince's signature "Cloud" guitar, to Les Paul's pioneering Log. The guitars have been chosen for this book either because they are great; or because they are significant; or because they look fantastic; or simply because they are downright weird.

1

EARLY
INSTRUMENTS

ALTHOUGH ITS ANCESTRY EXTENDS MANY THOUSANDS OF YEARS INTO THE PAST, IT WASN'T UNTIL THE SIXTEENTH CENTURY THAT THE GUITAR EMERGED IN A CLEARLY IDENTIFIABLE FORM. THIS CHAPTER FEATURES EXAMPLES OF SOME THE EARLIEST – AND MOST VISUALLY EXOTIC – GUITARS AND OTHER RELATED STRINGED INSTRUMENTS, WHICH WERE BUILT PRIOR TO THE TWENTIETH CENTURY.

LUTE 15TH CENTURY

Although the guitar in its recognised form began to emerge during the Renaissance, its origins are shrouded in some mystery – rather surprisingly since it can reasonably lay claim to be the world's most popular musical instrument. One common theory is that the guitar evolved from the European lute. Although the instruments are clearly related, the lute has a much longer history and the story is actually more complex. There is certainly evidence of guitar-like instruments having existed in Ancient Egypt and central Asia in pre-Christian times. But when looking back at the history of stringed instruments, even academics have barely been able to come to a consensus as to what actually constitutes a guitar.

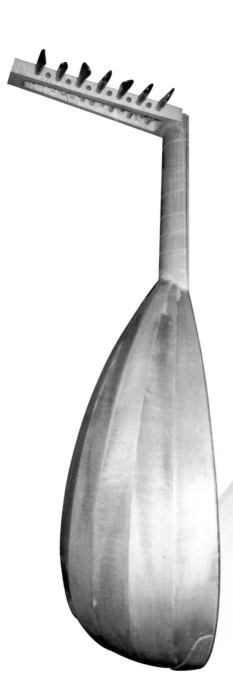

One immediate ancestor is the Gittern, a flat-backed, fretted instrument that emerged during the eleventh century. But although that description would seem to sound every bit like a modern acoustic guitar, by the time the first instruments were known by such name they owed much more in scale and construction to the lute.

Like the guitar, the lute is an ancestor of the Arabic *al ud*. Whether due to commerce or military activity, the ud was known to have reached Europe by the eleventh century. Slowly adapted by European craftsmen, by the early fifteenth century the lute had evolved.

The most distinctive feature of the instrument was the curved body shell, delicately fashioned from thin strips of maple or sycamore, and steamed so they could be bent into shape. In the early days of the lute, the soundboard was barely 2mm in thickness – a remarkable feat considering the crude tools available at the time. Indeed, they were so delicate that no lutes dating from before 1500 are known to have survived intact.

FIVE-COURSE
BAROQUE GUITAR
LATE 16TH-CENTURY

As lute-building techniques improved, new stronger structures made it possible to add an additional set of strings. Lutes had traditionally made use of four "courses", each course comprising a pair of strings tuned in unison.

One instrument to take advantage of these developments was the Spanish *vihuela*, a stringed instrument dating from the thirteenth century. A brief glance at even the oldest surviving example (of which there are very few) reveals the distinctive "figure-of-eight" body, which we now associate with the guitar, and a long neck. This is unlike the genuine "guitars" that emerged during this period, which were closer in scale to the lute.

The vihuela achieved its peak of popularity in the middle of the sixteenth century, when it was considered to be the instrument of choice among the musical élite. However, by the end of the century, it had been all but replaced by the five-course guitar. This did not please everybody, as can be seen from the work of one Sebastian Orosco, who wrote, shortly after the turn of the century: "…since the invention of the guitar there are very few who study the vihuela. This is a great loss because… the guitar is nothing but a cow-bell, so easy to play, especially when strummed, that there is not a stable-boy who is not a musician of the guitar."

FIVE-COURSE GUITAR

LATE 16TH-CENTURY

The first guitars were four-course instruments. They had waisted fronts, flat backs and sides and a fretted neck. And although much smaller, in many respects they resemble a modern classical guitar. The first mention of the guitar's "invention" appeared in 1487 in a work by Johannes Tinctoris in which he claimed that the instrument was "invented by the Catalans", the inhabitants of what is now north-east Spain.

In common with lutes of this period, the guitar was fitted with a rose over the sound hole. This was an ornately carved piece of wood. The frets were made of gut, which would be tied around the neck. The number of frets the guitar possessed would vary depending on the type of music to be played upon it. Simple strumming required no more than a handful of frets, whereas more complex music called for a greater number.

The five-course guitar appeared during the sixteenth century, and was essentially the same instrument with the addition of an extra course in the bass register. Again, it seems that the instrument originated in Spain and is likely to have been produced to satisfy the demands of the slightly more ambitious pieces being composed at that time.

STRADIVARI
GUITAR C.1680

And so it was that the very first guitars – both in
name and design – were established. Although these
early instruments were based heavily on the design of
the lute and the vihuela, it is clear that a new
instrument was beginning to emerge in its own right.
During the Baroque period (c.1600–1750), although
still overshadowed by the lute (which continued to be
the most popular plucked instrument) the five-course
guitar quickly replaced the four-course instrument, and
the vihuela gradually slid toward extinction.

One of the most striking features of Baroque guitars
is the incredibly ornate manner in which they tended to
be decorated. The sheer effort and care involved in
creating the beautiful designs with which these
instruments were adorned suggests a great passion
among those who possessed them. This was a period of
experimentation. Designs were achieved by staining the
different woods used in the guitar's construction. In
some cases, luthiers are known to have dispensed with
wood altogether, creating incredibly intricate inlaid
designs from tortoiseshell or ivory.

Among the most
outstanding examples of the art of the
guitar from this period are those produced by the
Voboam family, who were based in France, Joachim Tielke
in Germany and the Sellas brothers in Italy. Unusual among
guitar makers of the period were the guitars created by Antonio
Stradivari of Cremona, Italy. Universally known as the finest ever maker
of violins, Stradivari also made a small number of five-course guitars. His
instruments stand out for tasteful simplicity, with decoration limited to the
rose and soundhole surround, and a simple flourish either side of the
bridge. The back of the body (see across the page) resembles his violins
in the use of "curly" maple, the joins being inlaid with ebony.

Proof of the growing acceptance of the guitar can be found
in works composed for the instrument during the second
half of the seventeenth century. Italian Francesco
Corbetta was the instrument's leading composer of
the day. He composed "La Guitarre Royale" for King
Charles II, who made the instrument immediately
fashionable by taking it up himself. Some were
still not won over, though – noted diarist
Samuel Pepys wrote upon hearing Corbetta
play: "I was mightily troubled that so
much pains were taken on so bad
an instrument."

JEAN-BAPTISTE DE HAYE C.1800

By the end of the seventeenth century, Italy had become the undisputed centre of the guitar world. However, the instrument's popularity gradually spread north, through to Central Europe. When the Duchess Amalia von Weimar brought a five-string guitar from Italy to Weimar in 1788, this instrument became a template for some of the early guitars by the celebrated luthier Jacob August Otto. During the same period, composers such as Johann Arnold and Friedrich Baumbach helped to establish the instrument as a serious musical proposition.

In Holland and Belgium, the Cuypers family were the most eminent manufacturers of fine guitars. Very little is known about the luthier Jean Baptiste De Haye, however this instrument is a typical example of those being produced in Holland and France during this period.

JOSÉF PAGÉS C.1804

By the early 1800s, the number of strings or
courses used on most guitars had settled as six,
and what we now know as the standard
tuning of E-A-D-G-B-E became the norm.
At the same time, a new generation of
virtuoso players performed widely
throughout Europe, inspiring new
approaches to guitar construction. The
fingerboard was lengthened and raised
to improve playing in the upper
register: this required moving the
bridge to a more central position on
the soundboard. Luthiers such as Josef
Pagés and Louis Panormo began to
develop a rudimentary system of fan
struts to support the bridge in its new,
more vulnerable position.

This guitar was built by Pagés in around
1804 at his workshop in Cadiz, Southwest Spain.

THE "RIZZIO" GUITAR C.1680

This beautiful guitar was crafted in the late seventeenth century by Jean Baptiste Voboam (1648–1731), the son of the more eminent luthier René Voboam. The instrument also has a fascinating history in its own right: it was originally believed to have been owned and played by David Rizzio, secretary and advisor to Mary Stuart, Queen of Scots. Allegedly the Queen's lover, Rizzio was murdered in her presence at Holyrood Castle in 1566, apparently at the behest of her husband.

Now housed in the Royal College of Music collection in London, and known as "The Rizzio Guitar", its intricate construction and decoration are in themselves worthy of note. The body has a flat back with seven ribs in cypress or yew, inlaid with triple stripes of holly sandwiched between ebony. The sides are also in ebony with inlaid panel lines in holly and figured walnut. The neck, headstock and fingerboard also feature inlays of ebony.

Even by the standards of the period, the decoration is unusually ornate. The soundboard featured 16 repeating *fleur-de-lys* motifs radiating from the soundhole. The fingerboard and pegbox front are inlaid with a *quatrefeuille* design in mother-of-pearl and ebony. If we turn the guitar on its back, we see the intricate black-and-white chevron edgings characteristic of many of the Voboam family's guitars.

The fact that a courtier of such standing as Rizzio could be seen playing a guitar indicates that the instrument was gaining respect and fashionability, and was no longer considered to be a crude relative of the lute, fit only for peasant folk songs.

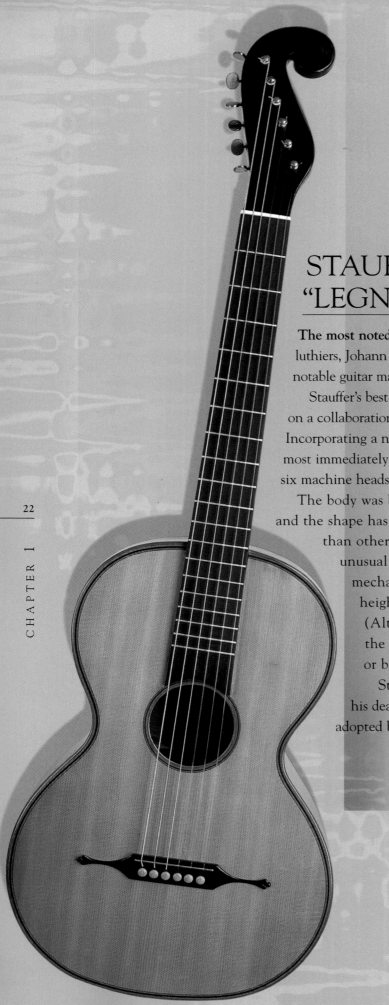

STAUFFER "LEGNANI" C.1820

The most noted of the Viennese school of nineteenth century luthiers, Johann Georg Stauffer (1778–1853) also trained other notable guitar makers such as Schertzer and C. F. Martin.

Stauffer's best-known instrument is the "Legnani" model, based on a collaboration with the Italian guitar virtuoso Luigi Legnani. Incorporating a number of innovative and influential features, the most immediately visible is the "Persian slipper" headstock, with all six machine heads positioned along one side.

The body was built from maple or rosewood with a spruce top and the shape has rather more exaggerated upper and lower bouts than other guitars of the time. The neck was particularly unusual in that it was adjustable: using a clock-key mechanism, the player was able raise and lower the height of the fingerboard to set the action.

(Altering the action on other "classical" guitars of the period required surgery to sand down the nut or bridge piece.)

Stauffer's influence was widespread. A century after his death, the "single-sided" headstock design was widely adopted by electric guitar makers.

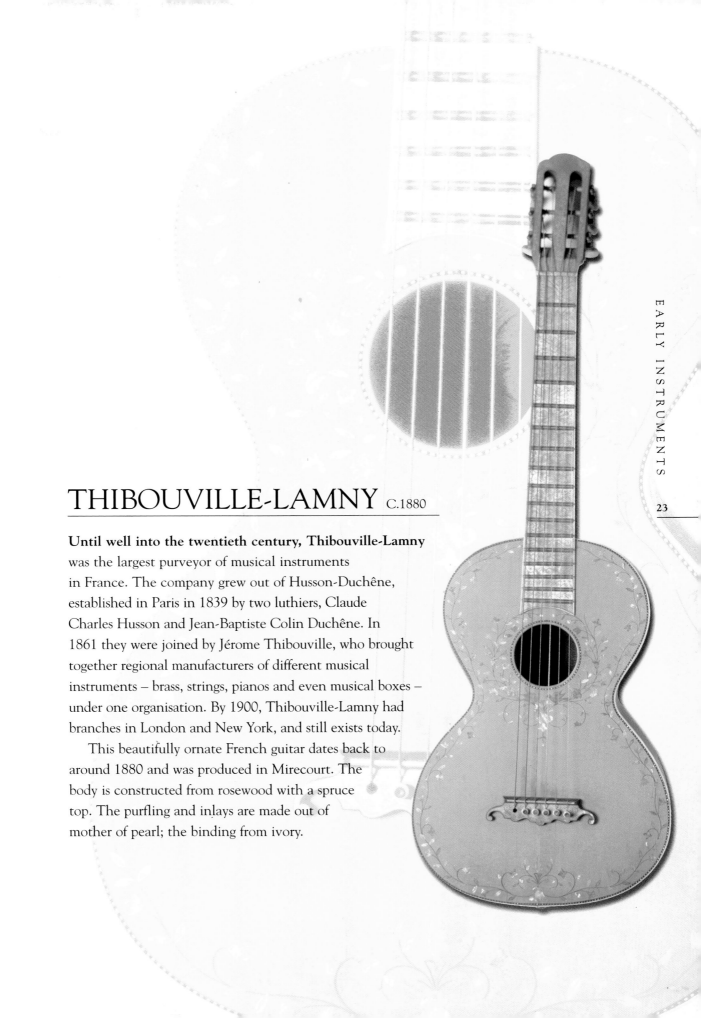

THIBOUVILLE-LAMNY C.1880

Until well into the twentieth century, Thibouville-Lamny was the largest purveyor of musical instruments in France. The company grew out of Husson-Duchêne, established in Paris in 1839 by two luthiers, Claude Charles Husson and Jean-Baptiste Colin Duchêne. In 1861 they were joined by Jérome Thibouville, who brought together regional manufacturers of different musical instruments – brass, strings, pianos and even musical boxes – under one organisation. By 1900, Thibouville-Lamny had branches in London and New York, and still exists today.

This beautifully ornate French guitar dates back to around 1880 and was produced in Mirecourt. The body is constructed from rosewood with a spruce top. The purfling and inlays are made out of mother of pearl; the binding from ivory.

THIBOUT
LYRE GUITAR C.1820

This rather unusual looking instrument is a guitar fashioned in the shape of an ancient Greek lyre. It dates back to the end of the eighteenth century when Europe (and in particular, France) enjoyed a so-called "classical revival". This particular instrument was made in around 1790 by Amadeé Thibout, of Caen (on the north coast of France).

Lyre guitars enjoyed a degree of popularity, but were evidently clumsy to play and somewhat lacking in sound quality. In 1806, Viennese composer and guitarist Simon Moliter said: "Its tone – though stronger than that of the guitar, on account of the larger body – is nevertheless dull and as though held back within the instrument."

Also popular during this period were so-called "harp guitars". These were multi-necked instruments with strings passing over a single soundhole. Gibson famously revived the idea in the 1920s.

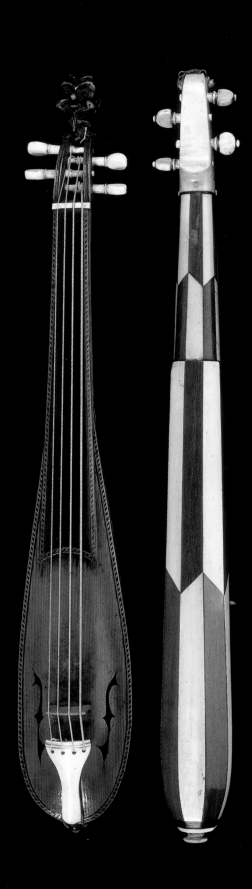

POCHE 1680

Not actually a guitar at all, but a small bowed instrument, the poche or Taschengeige is another European instrument to evolve directly from its Arabic counterpart – el rebec moresca. The instrument was widely used by dancing masters until the early nineteenth century. As its names suggest (*poche* is the French word for "pocket"; *taschengeige* literally translates as "bag violin"), the instrument was small enough to be carried in a pocket, and was played with a correspondingly small bow.

The instrument shown on the far left dates back to 1649, and was made by Matthias Hummel of Augsberg, German. It featured an ornate fingerboard carved from ebony and ivory. Hummel was also a noted lute maker.

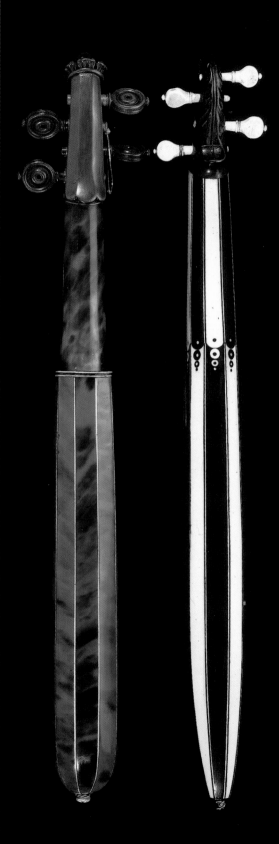

2

ACOUSTICS

THE PIONEERING WORK OF ANTONIO TORRES IN THE NINETEENTH-CENTURY CREATED A BLUEPRINT FOR THE MODERN CLASSICAL ACOUSTIC GUITAR. AT THE SAME TIME IN THE UNITED STATES, C. F. MARTIN WAS DESIGNING AN ACOUSTIC GUITAR THAT WAS TO GIVE BIRTH TO THE STEEL-STRING FOLK TRADITION, WHICH FOUND ITSELF AT THE HEART OF MUCH OF THE POPULAR MUSIC OF THE TWENTIETH CENTURY.

LOUIS PANORMO 1836

Louis Panormo was born in Paris in 1784,
the fourth son of an Italian luthier, Vincenzo
Panormo. He moved to London in 1819 and
set up shop in Bloomsbury, building
guitars, violins, cellos and double
basses. In shape and structure – in
particular his use of fan strutting –
his guitars were closely modelled on
those built by Joséf Pagés in Cadiz,
Spain at the end of the eighteenth
century. Indeed, his shop sign
boasted: "The only maker of guitars
in the Spanish style, 26 High Street
Bloomsbury, London. Guitars of every
description from 2 to 15 Guineas."
This example has a spruce top, a
bridge without a separate saddle, and a
finely carved headstock with large slots.
Panormo continued to work in
London until 1854, after which he
emigrated to join his son in New
Zealand. Louis was not the only
member of the family to make
musical instruments in
London. Two of his elder
brothers, Joseph and
George, and their
respective sons, Edward
and George Lewis, were
also successful luthiers.

CHRISTIAN FREDERICK MARTIN C. 1837

Hailing from a long line of musical instrument craftsmen, Christian Frederick Martin was born in 1796 in Germany. At the age of 15 he became apprenticed to the noted Viennese luthier Johann Stauffer.

In 1833, Martin emigrated to New York City, where he set up a modest music store that housed a small guitar production workshop in the back room.

Early Martin guitars were hand-crafted to order. Initially they were strongly reminiscent of the instruments he built for Stauffer back in Vienna, most notably in the headstock design, which featured all the tuning pegs positioned along one side. After six years of life in New York City – a place that Martin had never felt happy – he moved to Nazareth, Pennsylvania. Turning his back on retailing, Martin concentrated his efforts on the production of musical instruments. This guitar was built in Martin's New York City workshop and features an 18-fret fingerboard, rosewood body, spruce top and ornately decorated purfling around the edges.

TORRES C.1855

Antonio de Torres Jurado is the single most important figure in the evolution of what we now call the "classical" guitar.

Born in Almeria, Spain in 1817, the son of a tax collector, Torres began his working life as a carpenter. Moving to Granada in 1850, he learned his trade under the tuition of the luthier, Jose Pernas. Although little information exists about his time with Pernas, by all accounts, even his earliest efforts produced excellent results. A meeting with concert performer Julian Arcus evidently convinced Torres to dedicate his efforts exclusively to the guitar.

There are two definable "periods" of Torres' career as a luthier. The first phase begins in his workshop at Calle Cerregeria 32, in Seville in 1852 and ends in 1869. It was during this period that nearly all of his pioneering work took place.

Among his most celebrated instruments was *La Leona*, built in 1856. In 1858 he won a bronze medal in the Seville Exhibition for an extraordinarily decorated instrument in bird's eye maple.

Torres' most visibly dramatic development was in altering the proportions of the guitar, in particular elongating the body and "doming" the lower bout. He also experimented with materials. He firmly believed that the key to a guitar's sound was in its top, so he tried lighter and thinner woods. To give the instrument greater strength, he created a system of strutting on the underside

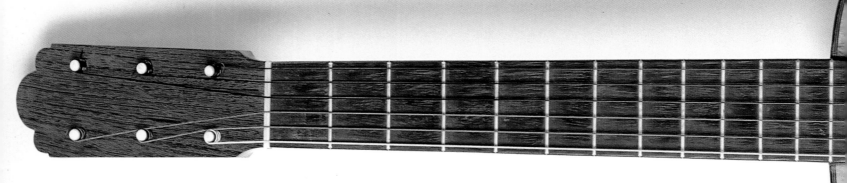

of the top. Although other earlier luthiers had used this approach, the seven "fan" struts developed by Torres gave the instrument greater strength and bass response.

The first guitarist to benefit from these new developments was the nineteenth century's greatest virtuoso, Francisco Tárrega. Performing widely in the concert halls of Europe, Tárrega evolved new playing techniques that resulted directly from Torres' work. Another notable client of the time was Miguel Llobert.

In spite of Tárrega's patronage, Torres was unable to make a good living as a luthier, and in 1870 he moved back to his native Almeria, where he opened a china shop. After 1875, he resumed guitar making, but on a part-time basis. Until his death in 1892 he produced around twelve guitars every year. Indeed, according to the biography written by José L. Romanillos *Antonio de Torres, Guitar Maker: His Life and Work* – a scholarly work from which most our knowledge of the man is derived – Torres manufactured only around 320 guitars during his lifetime, 66 of which are known to remain.

Numerous inventions connected to the guitar have been attributed to Torres over the years, but his real genius was less as an innovator than in his effectiveness at improving the most important developments of the day, and in doing so creating an instrument which has remained a template for the modern classical guitar.

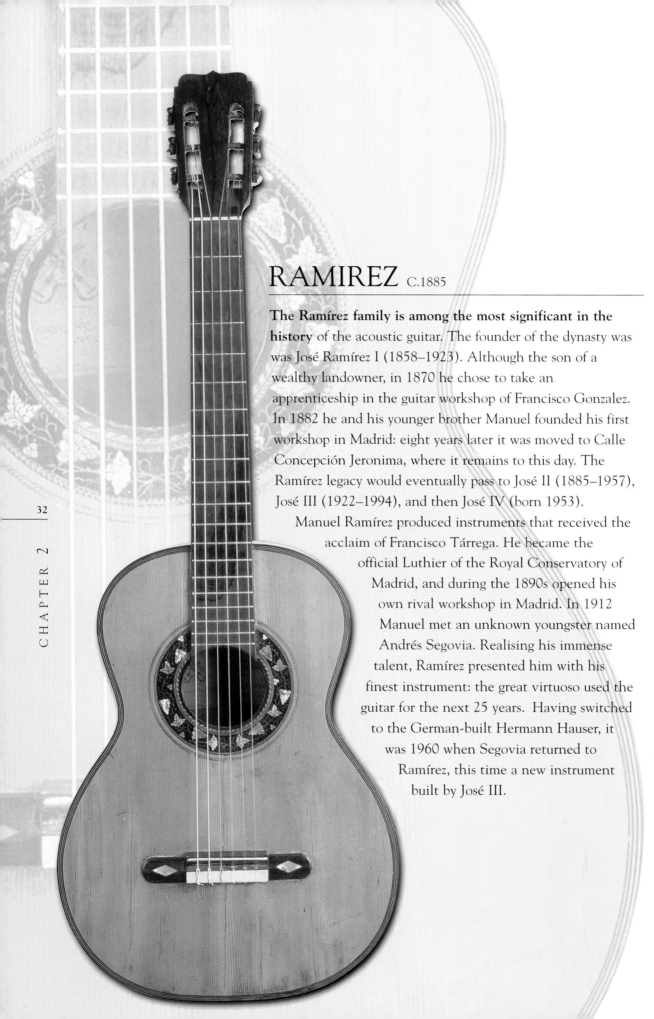

RAMIREZ C.1885

The Ramírez family is among the most significant in the history of the acoustic guitar. The founder of the dynasty was was José Ramírez I (1858–1923). Although the son of a wealthy landowner, in 1870 he chose to take an apprenticeship in the guitar workshop of Francisco Gonzalez. In 1882 he and his younger brother Manuel founded his first workshop in Madrid: eight years later it was moved to Calle Concepción Jeronima, where it remains to this day. The Ramírez legacy would eventually pass to José II (1885–1957), José III (1922–1994), and then José IV (born 1953).

Manuel Ramírez produced instruments that received the acclaim of Francisco Tárrega. He became the official Luthier of the Royal Conservatory of Madrid, and during the 1890s opened his own rival workshop in Madrid. In 1912 Manuel met an unknown youngster named Andrés Segovia. Realising his immense talent, Ramírez presented him with his finest instrument: the great virtuoso used the guitar for the next 25 years. Having switched to the German-built Hermann Hauser, it was 1960 when Segovia returned to Ramírez, this time a new instrument built by José III.

SALVADOR IBANEZ
LATE 19TH CENTURY

Salvador Ibanez was a highly rated luthier who spent his entire working life based in the Spanish city of Valencia. This beautiful instrument has a rosewood body with a spruce top, with highly ornate mother-of-pearl chevron inlays.

Surprisingly perhaps, the guitar belonged to Eric Clapton, and was sold in 1999 along with many other instruments from his vast collection, in aid of his Crossroads Centre charity. This guitar alone raised over $48,000. According to Clapton's long-serving technician Lee Dixon: "Eric often likes a gut-strung guitar to warm up with… he really liked it… it's been on the sessions for a couple of records."

GIBSON L-5 1922

Although it was C. F. Martin and his ancestors who established the US as the home of most of the important post-Torres innovations, it was Orville Gibson who founded the company that would not only provide an alternative tradition to the flat-top acoustic guitar, but would later play a crucial role during the transition to the electric era.

The son of a British immigrant, during the 1880s Gibson began producing a range of beautifully carved mandolins using methods of construction more usually applied to violins. The principal difference was in the intricately curved tops with the bridge and saddles positioned across the apex. During the following decade, Gibson applied the same ideas to his guitars, which became known as "archtops".

Surprisingly, perhaps, after Orville Gibson's death in 1918, the company began to flourish, and was responsible for a a number of developments that would have a major impact on the future of the guitar.

Steered by the innovative research of Lloyd Loar, in 1922, Gibson launched the first in a succession of historically important production archtop guitars – the Gibson L-5.

Among this instrument's unusual features was the replacement of the conventional circular soundhole with two violin-style tuned "f-holes". This, along with the "Virzitone" sound producer built into the body, helped to create a strong, full, warm sound which was able to project chord work through the brass-dominated dance bands of the period. It could even be said to have influenced the very course of American popular music – with the capability of producing greater volume, the L-5 was so successful that by the end of the decade it had all but replaced the banjo and ukulele in dance bands. Indeed, many of the early pioneers of jazz guitar used a Gibson L-5.

GIBSON SJ-200 1937

The SJ-200 is significant in that, unlike most previous
Gibson acoustic guitars, its top is flat rather than arched.
Gibson had experimented with the idea of "flat-tops" since
the early 1920s, but it was the success of the Martin
"Dreadnought" series that drove the company to produce
a more seriously considered model. Consequently, in 1934,
Gibson produced their first "jumbo" model. This
was followed three years later by the even
larger-bodied "Super Jumbo", the SJ-200.
The prototype model was built for the
famed Hollywood "singing cowboy", Ray
Whitley. Squarely designed to compete
with Martin guitars, the SJ-200 was built
with the country musician in mind – this
is self-evident from the cow's horn "moustache"
bridge and ornate detailing of the
scratchplate and fingerboard inlays.
Gibson were typically immodest
about their new creation: "The
King of the Flat-top Guitars,"
so proclaimed the advertising
literature.

SELMER MACCAFERRI 1932

One of the most fascinating figures in the development of the twentieth century guitar, Mario Maccaferri was not only an innovative luthier but a celebrated guitarist.

Maccaferri was born in Bologna, Italy in 1900, and at the age of eleven he became apprenticed to the Italian master luthier and musician, Luigi Mozzani, where he concurrently pursued the study of guitar making and playing. Graduating with the highest honours from the Sienna Conservatory, he embarked upon a successful concert career. In 1929, Maccaferri settled in London where, in between touring and teaching, he began to conceive of an instrument that combined a smooth tone with a high volume. By 1932 Selmer of Paris was producing his design.

The most striking visual feature of the Selmer Maccaferri is the perpendicular cutaway in the upper bout that allows easy access to the upper register. The guitar's distinctive tone and high volume was created by a revolutionary internal sound chamber built into the body. However, following a dispute with Henri Selmer, production ceased within a year.

Fewer than three hundred of these guitars were originally made. Popularised by the great European jazz guitarist Django Reinhardt, the Maccaferri is now highly prized by guitar collectors.

DOBRO "RESONATOR" 1934

As the guitar became more widely used for ensemble
playing, the most significant trend among luthiers of the
1920s was to produce instruments capable of generating
a higher volume. One of the most innovative solutions
was developed by the Dopyera Brothers, a family of four
Slovakian immigrants living in California – it was the
so-called "Resonator" guitar.

The acoustic principle on which it worked was similar
to an audio loudspeaker. The Dopyeras fitted a floating
aluminium cone into the top of a regular guitar, and
attached it to the bridge. Whenever a string was struck
the vibrations were passed through the bridge saddles
and transferred to the cone, which "resonated" back and

forth. The sound it created was a rather harsh,
distinctive metallic jangle, but it was nonetheless much
louder than any other acoustic guitar of the time.

The earliest resonator guitars were built in 1926 for
the National Guitar Company, in which one of the
Dopyera brothers – Louis – had invested. The following
year, however, the other three brothers – John, Rudy
and Ed – broke away to build guitars for their own
Dobro company. The main difference between
instruments produced by the two companies was that
Nationals not only featured aluminium resonators, but
aluminium bodies; whereas Dobros had the aluminium
cone fitted into regular flat-top acoustic guitars.

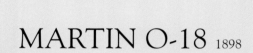

MARTIN O-18 1898

After the death of C.F. Martin in 1873, the company continued successfully under the guidance of successive generations of the family. However, it was under the presidency of Martin's grandson, Frank Henry, that some of the company's most innovative products were developed.

    Slowly evolving across the ages, the Martin "Style 18" – first launched in 1857 – is one of the simplest offered by the company, with very little in the way of decoration.

MARTIN O-45 1904

The famous Martin O-45 was introduced in 1904. The body is made of rosewood with a spruce soundboard.

Martin guitars are categorised by their styles and body shapes.
Body shapes:

O	Concert size
OO	Grand concert size
OOO	Auditorium size
D	Dreadnought size
DS	Dreadnought with 12-frets to the body
M	Grand auditorium size
MC	Grand auditorium with cutaway body
OM	Orchestra model
C	Classical
N	Classical (European)
F	F-hole model

Major styles:

16- Spruce top, quarter-sawn mahogany back and sides, slotted headstock, wide rosewood fingerboard, no fret markers or fingerplate.

18- 14-frets to the body, solid headstock, white dot position markers, "belly" bridge, dark edgings and fingerplate.

28- Rosewood back and sides, spruce top, and white edging

45- Spruce soundboard, rosewood back and side, ebony fingerboard, and abalone pearl inlays.

MARTIN D-18
THE "ELVIS" GUITAR 1935

The D-18 is one of Martin's noted range of large-bodied "Dreadnought" instruments. Owned and used by Elvis Presley between 1953 and 1955, this 1942 model is arguably one of the most famous guitars of the twentieth century.

This was the period when Elvis, electric guitarist Scotty Moore, bassist Bill Black, and drummer DJ Fontana, created their revolutionary rockabilly sound for Sun Records in Memphis, Tennessee. For many, this is where rock 'n' roll was born.

Now considered one the Martin company's greatest innovations, the Dreadnought guitar took over twenty years to evolve from prototype to production line. Frank Henry Martin had come up with the notion of building a large-bodied guitar in conjunction with a man named Harry Hunt, who worked for the Ditson music store in New York. Named after the First World War British battleship, the Ditson Dreadnought was constructed with a wide waist and narrow sloping shoulders. This new instrument was capable of producing a high volume and powerful bass response, making it an ideal accompaniment for vocalists.

In spite of Martin's pivotal role in its birth, the first Dreadnoughts were available exclusively from the Ditson store. In 1928 Ditsons went out of business and the Martin design team began to experiment with their own Dreadnought models. Strengthening the neck and replacing the traditional classical fan-bracing system with Martin's own "X-brace", the prototype D-1 and D-2 models were built.

The first genuine Martin Dreadnoughts went into general production in 1935 – these are the classic D-18 and D-28 styles. The best-known Dreadnought is the legendary Martin D-45, which was originally built in 1933 as a one-off for singing cowboy Gene Autry.

Since this important innovation, virtually every significant guitar manufacturer has produced its own alternative to the Dreadnought.

GIBSON EVERLY BROTHERS 1962

During the early 1960s, America's leading pop vocal duo The Everly Brothers – Don and Phil – enjoyed worldwide hits with such classics of the era as "Dream", "Wake Up Little Susie" and "Ebony Eyes". In 1962, Gibson launched a signature model for the duo.

In shape, the guitar was similar to the earlier Gibson J-185, although with a slightly thinner body. One feature that makes the "Everly" highly visually distinctive is the enormous tortoiseshell pickguard which, unusually, extends to both the treble and bass bouts – and indeed covers most of the top of the instrument. The rosewood fingerboard is also notable for its rather neat star-shaped markers, inlaid in mother-of-pearl.

In 1972, with the Everly Brothers now well out of vogue (and no longer even talking to each other), Gibson ended production. A reissue model with an inferior specification was offered in 1986.

ELVIS ARCHTOP C.1955

This "no-name" German archtop acoustic would hardly be noteworthy had it not been played by one of pop's greatest celebrities.

During his time in the US Army, Elvis Presley turned down many requests from high-ranking officials to perform, claiming – quite truthfully – that such things were restricted by his recording and managerial contracts. However, he is known to have performed privately on many occasions for fellow servicemen.

In 1959, at a party during winter manoeuvres in the south of what was then West Germany, Elvis met a young GI named Robert Allison. Elvis's presence at social gatherings always created a stir, and – as always – he was asked if he'd sing a few tunes. Having refused earlier in the evening citing his usual reasons, on this occasion Elvis changed his mind. Borrowing Allison's guitar, he gave impromptu renditions of "Love Me Tender" and "Don't Be Cruel". Before leaving the party he provided a very personal souvenir, signing the guitar "To 'Bob' Robert, Don't try too hard, thanks from Elvis Presley".

GIBSON HUMMINGBIRD 1960

With its ornately carved scratchplate, the Hummingbird was near the top of Gibson's flat-top line – second in cost only to the J-200.

Launched in 1960, the Hummingbird was Gibson's first square-shouldered "dreadnought-style" instrument.

This 1963 model was owned by Keith Richards, and used on many of the Rolling Stones' classic albums of the 1960s.

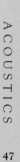

EPIPHONE
FT112 BARD 1969

The Epiphone brand name was taken over by
Gibson in 1957, and until around 1970, all
Epiphones were built at Gibson's factory in
Kalamazoo, Michigan.

During the 1960s, a number of high-
quality steel-strung, Epiphone flat-tops
appeared, of which the Excellente and Bard
models were at the top of the range.

This FT112 Bard twelve-string was used
by Eric Clapton during his time with the
pioneering heavy rock "supergroup" Cream.
The scratchplate displays the
characteristic epiphone "crossed E".

GUILD F47 1969

Guild guitars was founded in New York City in 1952 by music store owner Alfred Dronge, who put together a small team of experienced luthiers with the specific aim of producing limited quantities of hand-built, high-performance acoustic and electric guitars. An ex-professional guitarist, Dronge used his former contacts to test out new instruments, thus helping to establish a reputation for the brand.

Guild expanded rapidly during the early 1960s,

becoming a public company, and moving to new factory premises in Hoboken, New Jersey. Here they produced their first flat-top acoustic instruments to cater for the folk boom of the period.

In 1995, Guild was acquired by the ever-growing Fender Corporation, and although it still produces a complete range of guitars, it is on its top-end acoustic and electric acoustic instruments – such as the F47 shown here – that its reputation now rests.

ESTESO FLAMENCO GUITAR 1934

Flamenco is the native music of Andalucia, in the South of Spain. Although standard classical models have often been used for flamenco, specialised flamenco guitars began to appear during the early part of the twentieth century. These were lighter than classical instruments, with the action set lower to aid faster playing and create a percussive sound. Since flamenco playing often involves the tapping of the body with the fingernails, a *golpeador* (tap plate) was often attached to protect the finish. Domingo Esteso was one of the most noted flamenco guitar makers. Born in 1882, he trained under Manuel Ramirez before setting up his own acclaimed Madrid workshop in 1915. Among his early clients was Sabicas, the greatest of the pre-war flamenco players. When Esteso died in 1937, his business was taken over by his apprenticed nephews, Faustino, Mariano and Julio Conde. *Los Hermanos Conde* carried on the Esteso tradition. Indeed, his original workshop in Calle Gravina, Madrid, continues to produce fine acoustic guitars.

3

EARLY ELECTRICS

AWAY FROM THE CLASSICAL ARENA, MUSIC WAS BEING PLAYED AT INCREASINGLY HIGH VOLUMES. AS A CONSEQUENCE, GUITARISTS FOUND IT HARD TO COMPETE WITH OTHER LOUDER INSTRUMENTS. A SOLUTION EMERGED IN THE 1920s WHEN MAGNETIC PICKUPS MADE IT POSSIBLE TO AMPLIFY THE GUITAR'S SOUND. THIS DEVELOPMENT WOULD HAVE UNTOLD REPERCUSSIONS ON THE WAY MUSIC WAS TO EVOLVE.

RO-PAT-IN "FRYING PAN" 1931

No single figure can be credited with "inventing" the electric guitar. Instead, we find ourselves with a disparate group of far-sighted individuals, all of whom made their own important contributions to what eventually become the most influential musical instrument of the twentieth century.

In 1919, Gibson hired Lloyd Loar to head their Kalamazoo engineering and research departments. During his five years with the company he made a huge impact on those around him. Not content with overseeing the creation of the revolutionary L5 guitar, he was perhaps the first person to experiment with the

idea of using a magnetic pickup to amplify stringed instruments. His first designs were for an electric double bass – there have even been claims that he produced a crude electric guitar during this period. Sadly, it soon became evident that Loar's ideas were too futuristic for the notoriously conservative Gibson, and he went his own way. During the 1930s, Loar's own Vivi-Tone company would produced some of the first true electrified guitars.

The second significant character in the story was a charismatic Texan named George Beauchamp. Initially a partner of the Dopyera brothers, and one of the

creators of the "Dobro" resonator guitar, in 1931, he teamed up with designer Paul Barth and toolmaker Adolph Rickenbacker to form the Ro-Pat-In Company. Together they produced an electrified lap-steel "Hawaiian" guitar. Because of its distinctive shape, it quickly became known as the "Frying Pan". The instrument first went into production under the Ro-Pat-In brand name, but was soon replaced by the Rickenbacker brand.

The Frying Pan was powered by a pair of large horse-shoe magnets that passed under the strings. The body and neck of the prototype models were made from a single piece of maple, however by the time they became publicly available cast aluminium was used instead. This was not entirely successful, since the use of aluminium evidently resulted in problems keeping the instrument in tune. Later in the decade Rickenbacker produced lap-steels made from strong bakelite plastic which proved to be more successful. Variations on the "Frying Pan" design remained available until well into the 1950s.

Although not guitars in the conventional sense, these were the first commercially produced electric instruments. (Although, the Dopyera brothers – with whom George Beauchamp had earlier parted company with some acrimony – would later claim that they produced an electrified National earlier than the Frying Pan.)

For many modern guitarists, the idea that their electrified instruments owe their heritage to such a "minority" instrument, may seem strange. The reason is simply that Hawaiian music was extremely popular in the US during this time, and, for a brief period, the lap steel was more popular than the "Spanish" guitar.

RICKENBACKER ELECTRO SPANISH 1935

The Rickenbacker Electro Spanish guitar of 1935 was built using Bakelite, a synthetic resin developed by a Belgian chemist in the early part of the twentieth century. It featured a bolt-on neck with 23 integral frets:

the Electro may have been the first guitar to feature such a neck joint. The horseshoe-magnet pickup is essentially the same as the one fitted to the Frying Pan.

Of particular interest here is the patented Vibrola tailpiece, designed by Doc Kauffman which featured on both the Electro Spanish, and its Hawaiian "partner", the Electro Spanish B. The Vibrola unit has a short handle that can be adjusted for length. When

VIB-ROLA
PAT NO.1839395

pushed downward, it lowers the pitch of the strings – when released, spring tension brings the strings back to regular pitch.

The Electro Spanish guitar was not a popular instrument – probably due to its small ukulele-size body and heavy weight. Although the Electro Spanish model was discontinued after several years of production, its Hawaiian counterpart stayed in production well into the 1950s.

An argument could be made for the Electro being the first commercially produced, solid-body electric guitar. For although removal of the screw-fitted dome covers on the top of the body revealed a series of hollowed-out chambers, they were not created for acoustic reasons, but for the sake of efficient mould design, and to reduce weight and material used. At the very least, this was an important instrument in the on-going electrification of the guitar.

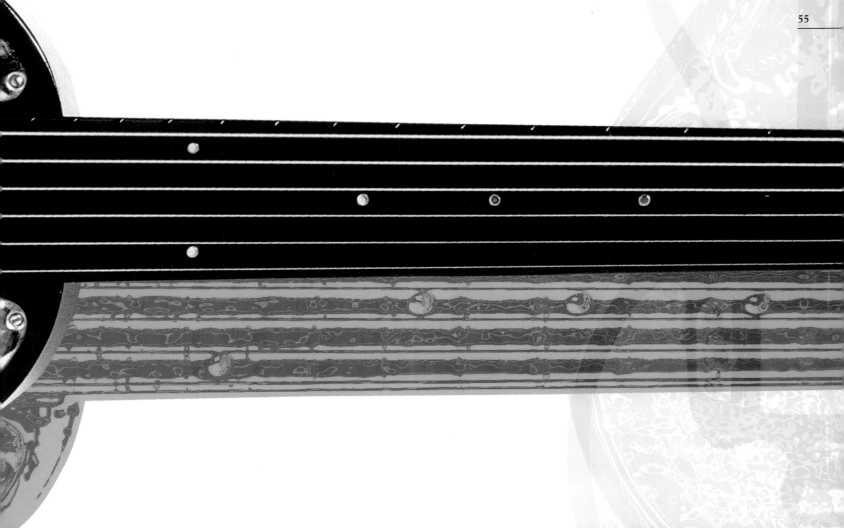

GIBSON ES-150 1936

Gibson's Lloyd Loar may have played a pioneering role in the electrification of the guitar, but the early commercial running had been made by small-scale operators. At this time, interest in electric instruments was largely attributable to novelty: few established guitarists took them seriously. All of this changed in 1936 when the mighty Gibson company produced their first dedicated production-line electric guitar, the ES-150.

In 1934, Walter Fuller was hired by Gibson to resurrect the idea of producing an electric guitar. His pickup design comprised two solid nickel magnets mounted on a steel bar and surrounded by a coil. It provided a basic blueprint for all the pickups that followed. This was fitted beneath the strings of a standard L-50 archtop acoustic.

Marketed in their trade catalogue as "Another Miracle from Gibson", the ES-150 was the first electric guitar to go into large-scale production. The success of the instrument could be largely attributed to the patronage of a number of high-profile players – most notably jazz legend Charlie Christian. For the first time, the electrical guitar could be regarded as a serious musical proposition.

GIBSON
SUPER 400 CES 1951

Gibson had pioneered the manufacture of large-bodied archtop acoustic guitars since the birth of the L5 in the 1920s. Launched in 1934, the Super 400 was the largest acoustic instrument the company made.

The electric Super 400 CES (or "Super 4" as it's often called) arrived in 1951. An instrument capable of polarising musicians, for some the Super 4's sheer size ($4^1/_2$ inches deep and 18 inches wide) is too bulky and awkward to hold; for others – among them jazz players such as Larry Coryell and Kenny Burrell – the body volume proved one of the keys to its deep mellow sound.

Although the instrument is still in production, rare 1950s models currently change hands for very large sums of money.

GIBSON ES-175 1949

By the start of the 1940s, Gibson had assumed pole position as far as the electric guitar market was concerned. By far the biggest-selling electric guitar of the 1930s, the ES-150 had been a down-the-line, gimmick-free instrument. However, for all of its success, essentially it was merely a high-quality acoustic guitar with an attached pickup.

In 1944, Gibson was taken over by the Chicago Musical Instrument Company (CMI). Foreseeing an unprecedented demand for guitars after the end of World War Two, a new young President, Ted McCarty, was brought in, with a brief to concentrate on a new line of electric models. In 1949, Gibson unleashed the ES-175 – a guitar specifically designed as an electric instrument, rather than an acoustic with a pickup.

Although launched as a economy
instrument, construction of the ES-175 remained typical of
the Gibson tradition. The hollow body features a "Florentine" cutaway
and two "f-holes"; the front and back are cut from pressed maple plywood, with
solid maples sides. The neck was made from mahogany with a pressed rosewood
fingerboard.

The original ES-175 featured a single P90 pickup with individually
adjustable polepieces – this effectively allows the volume of each
string to be tweaked in relation to the overall volume. Other
pickup options have become available over the years.

The ES-175 has stayed in production ever since, becoming
one of Gibson's biggest selling guitars. Its rich tone
continues to find favour, particularly
among jazz players.

LES PAUL "LOG" 1941

The Gibson ES-150 was a milestone in the story of the guitar. Not only were jazz musicians such as Charlie Christian turned on to the potential of the electric guitar, but emerging country stars such as Chet Atkins and Merle Travis, or bluesmen like Muddy Waters and Elmore James.

A fundamental problem of the early electric guitars – which were, after all, little more than acoustic guitars with pickups fitted – was that if the amplifier volume was too great, sound from the loudspeaker could easily cause the body of the guitar and strings to vibrate on their own. This created a howling noise referred to as "feedback".

Whilst rock players in the 1960s began to harness this sound as a part of their playing technique, to the early electric players it was merely a nuisance. The logical solution to this problem was to increase the body mass of the instrument: without a working soundbox the guitar's capacity for vibration would be greatly reduced. From the beginning of the 1940s, a number of generally unrelated parties set about designing and building a solid-body electric guitar that would achieve this end.

No-one can truly say who produced the first purpose-built solid-body electric guitar but there are a number of candidates whose research work was unquestionably important. Designer-engineers Lloyd Loar and O.W. Appleton are known to have at least experimented with solid bodies while developing magnetic pickups.

One clear candidate is country-jazz guitarist Les Paul. Born Lester William Polfus, as a musician, he is best-remembered for easy listening hits of the late 1940s accompanying his wife, Mary Ford. However, it is his signature on one of the most famous guitars ever made that will guarantee his immortality. A keen inventor from an early age, Paul was given full access to the Epiphone workshop by owner and friend Epi Stathopoulo. Here he created his own "Log" guitar using a Gibson neck attached to a solid piece of pine on which the pickups and bridge were mounted – the bouts from an Epiphone hollow-body archtop were added to the side to give the guitar a broadly normal appearance.

In 1949 he took his prototype to Maurice Berlin, the president of Gibson's parent company, CMI. As Paul remembers: "He said 'Forget it'. He called it a broomstick." Within two years he was called back.

In 1947,

engineer Paul Bigsby produced a

solid-body instrument designed in conjunction
with country guitarist Merle Travis. Bigsby and Travis had
first collaborated three years earlier when the guitarist had requested
some improvements be made to the vibrola on his Gibson guitar. Bigsby
came up with a completely new design for a vibrato arm, which would be widely
used over the next twenty years. This Bigsby–Travis guitar represented an
important development for a number of reasons. The shape of the body and headstock
was clearly influential – some of the lines are clearly echoed in the early Fender and
Gibson guitars that followed over the next decade. So, too, was the thinline "bird's-eye"
maple body and the fact that it featured a "straight-through" neck.

Since at least a dozen of these instruments were produced, the Bigsby Merle Travis could
lay a reasonable claim to having been the first "production" solid-body electric guitar.

BIGSBY MERLE TRAVIS 1947

4

FENDERS

ALTHOUGH LEO FENDER COULD NOT CLAIM TO HAVE INVENTED THE SOLID-BODY ELECTRIC GUITAR, WHEN HE TOOK A PRODUCTION-LINE APPROACH TO MANUFACTURING THE BROADCASTER IN 1950, NOTHING LESS THAN A MUSICAL REVOLUTION WAS BORN. IN 1954, HE DESIGNED AND LAUNCHED THE LEGENDARY STRATOCASTER – THE MOST FAMOUS ELECTRIC GUITAR EVER MADE.

FENDER BROADCASTER 1950

It's difficult to overestimate the significance of the
launch of the Fender Broadcaster in 1950, not only to the
evolution of the electric guitar, but to the music that would
emerge over the decades that followed.

The Broadcaster was by no means a work of startling
originality: the pioneering efforts to create a solid-body electric
guitar had been worked out a decade earlier by the likes of Les
Paul, Merle Travis and Paul Bigsby. The genius of Leo Fender and
his engineer George Fullerton was to conceive a production-line
approach to electric guitar manufacture. In the past, guitar
makers had been master craftsmen; Fender sought to demystify
the process.

The Broadcaster dispensed with the complex contours
associated with traditional archtop guitars, its body a simple
slab of solid ash that – as Fender's early critics decried –
could be cut out and fashioned by anyone who owned a
buzz-saw. But this was precisely the point: everything
about the Broadcaster was basic, from its minimalistic
body shape to the simple bridge pickup
construction. The maple neck was not precision-
glued to the body, but was bolted on using four
self-tapping screws. The electronic circuitry was
mounted on the inside of a chrome plate, which
was itself secured to the body with a pair of
screws. Such simplicity was well-suited to the
production line, and also meant that any part of
the guitar could be easily replaced in the event
of damage. Fender's aim was to mass-produce an
electric guitar at an affordable price. As such,
the Fender Broadcaster was a critical landmark.

CHAPTER 4

FENDER TELECASTER 1951

Early in 1951, Leo Fender was advised that his use of the name
Broadcaster had infringed a copyright – the New York Gretsch instrument
company had long been producing a range of drums using the name
"Broadkaster". To avoid litigation, from February 1951, the
Broadcaster transfers on the headstock of unsold guitars were
scratched off, leaving just the Fender logo. (These so-called
"No-casters" are now highly prized collectibles.) It was Fender
employee, Don Randall, who came up with a new name.
Post-war America having rapidly fallen under the spell
of television, he sought a word that would make a clear
connection: the Fender Telecaster was born – a modern
instrument for the modern world.

Most early sales of the Broadcaster/Telecaster were made
at bandstands or direct from the factory, but word soon spread.
Initially favoured by country musicians, the "Tele" would quickly
find a home in every possible future musical genre.

Although Telecasters are most often seen in their traditional
"blond" or natural finishes, a number of alternatives have appeared
over the years. In the late 1960s, Fender paid homage to the
psychedelic era with a limited run in "Paisley Red" – this effect was
achieved by pasting wallpaper to the body before varnishing. The
Telecaster has also appeared in a number of variations, among
them the lighter, hollow-body Thinline, and the souped-up
Elite, featuring humbucking pickups and active circuitry.

The first production-line solid-body electric guitar, the
Telecaster has been in production ever since, and remains
an undisputed classic instrument.

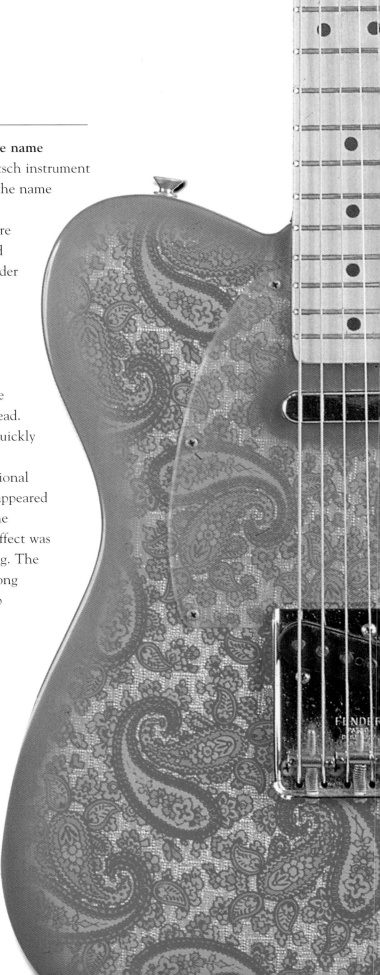

FENDER JAMES BURTON TELECASTER 1990

The late 1980s saw the beginning of a new trend in guitar marketing – instruments bearing the signature of a well-known musician. In 1988, Eric Clapton asked Fender to produce a custom Stratocaster with a heavily compressed pickup sound and a neck like his favourite 1930s Martin acoustic guitar. Fender not only obliged, but made the resulting Eric Clapton Stratocaster – complete with Old Slowhand's signature alongside the Fender logo – available to the general public. It was so successful that others soon followed. Players that would soon be similarly honoured by Fender included Yngwie Malmsteen, Robert Cray, Stevie Ray Vaughan, Albert Collins, Danny Gatton and James Burton.

Like most of the guitarists in that list, James Burton is not exactly a household name, but he is unquestionably a "guitarist's guitarist". One of America's greatest session players, Burton's tasteful country picking style has backed everyone from Ricky Nelson and Emmylou Harris to Elvis Presley. A prominent Telecaster user, he was an obvious choice as a signatory to this supercharged model that hit the production line in 1990. Although the basic guitar is Telecaster through and through, it makes use of features more usually associated with the Stratocaster. Most notably, the characteristic two pickups have been replaced by three Lace Sensor pickups and a five-way selector switch. Furthermore, the traditional chrome fittings on the bridge, headstock have been replaced by gold plating.

Arguably the Rolls–Royce of Telecasters, the James Burton model offered substantial improvements to a classic instrument without compromising the characteristics that first made it great.

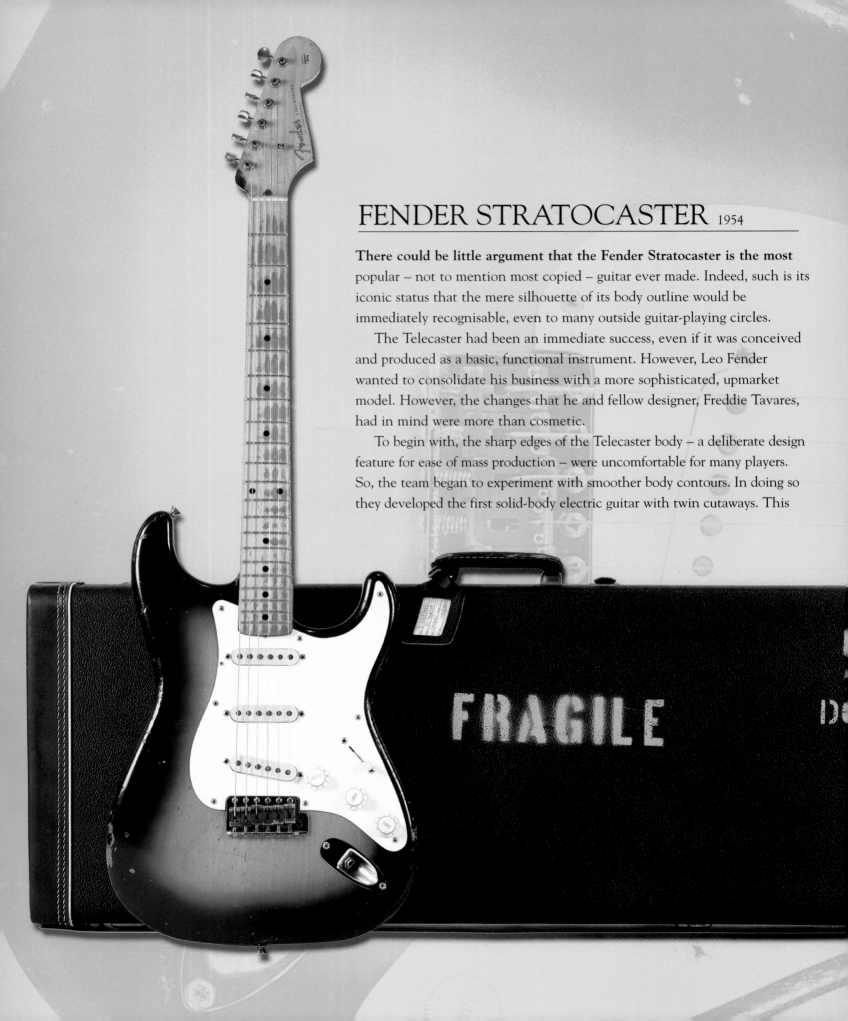

FENDER STRATOCASTER 1954

There could be little argument that the Fender Stratocaster is the most popular – not to mention most copied – guitar ever made. Indeed, such is its iconic status that the mere silhouette of its body outline would be immediately recognisable, even to many outside guitar-playing circles.

The Telecaster had been an immediate success, even if it was conceived and produced as a basic, functional instrument. However, Leo Fender wanted to consolidate his business with a more sophisticated, upmarket model. However, the changes that he and fellow designer, Freddie Tavares, had in mind were more than cosmetic.

To begin with, the sharp edges of the Telecaster body – a deliberate design feature for ease of mass production – were uncomfortable for many players. So, the team began to experiment with smoother body contours. In doing so they developed the first solid-body electric guitar with twin cutaways. This

gave the player unprecedented access to the highest notes on the fingerboard, as well as creating both a balanced look and feel.

In terms of functionality, there was even greater ambition. The Telecaster bridge unit had featured three independent string saddles, each one controlling the height and length of a pair of strings; Fender began to investigate the idea of using six, fully adjustable saddles, making it possible for each string to be adjusted independently. Furthermore, although the twin pickups of the Telecaster were capable of creating very different sounds, a third, middle pickup would surely provide even greater versatility. Some Telecaster players had also complained about the ease at which their connecting leads became detached from their guitars, so Fender gave the new model a jack-plug socket recessed in the front of the body. Finally, a vibrato arm was provided as a standard feature.

Whereas the Telecaster derived its name from the popularity of the new TV medium, Fender's new guitar played on a fast-growing national obsession with space exploration. With the Stratocaster a true star was born.

After a long association with Gibson guitars, Eric Clapton acquired his first Stratocaster in 1967. The model shown here – dubbed "Brownie" – was used on the 1970 rock classic "Layla" by Derek and the Dominos. He also played a composite Strat which he constructed himself. This was famously known as "Blackie".

FENDER STRATOCASTER 1954

The first Stratocasters off the assembly line appeared in a two-tone "sunburst". However, from 1956, buyers had the choice of a variety of custom colour finishes, making it possible to own Fenders in such exotic shades as Surf Green, Shoreline Gold and Fiesta Red.

During the early 1960s, Leo Fender became concerned about a long-standing health problem, and decided to sell his company. By the end of 1964, when the Columbia Broadcasting System (CBS) bought the company for $13 million, it was exporting more instruments to the rest of the world than all its US competitors put together. The inevitable corporate rationalisation that followed came at a price, however, and the quality of Fender guitars diminished. Even now, "pre-CBS" Fenders are highly prized among vintage guitar collectors.

The instrument shown here is the 1968 model used so spectacularly by Jimi Hendrix at the 1969 Woodstock Festival. Fender Sales Director Dale Hyatt would later quip: "I think Jimi Hendrix caused more Stratocasters to be sold than all the Fender salesmen put together!"

There have been cheap
Japanese imitations of the classic
Fenders in production since the 1960s.
At first, these models were of such low quality that
they posed no commercial threat. By the 1980s, however,
competitors such as Tokai were producing Strat-like guitars that
were almost as good as the real thing. Fender responded in 1983
with the launch of the Squier diffusion brand,
producing Japanese-made, low-cost, high-quality
guitars. Over time the company began to
manufacture cheaper instruments bearing the
Fender logo in Japan and Mexico. The American
models remain the most revered, but many players –
even professionals – now make little distinction.

FENDER STRATOCASTER 1990

FENDER JAZZMASTER 1958

The success
of the Telecaster and the
Stratocaster overshadowed many
other fine Fender electric guitars.
Launched in 1958, the Jazzmaster was the
company's top-of-the-line model, initially retailing
at $329 – some $50 more than the Strat.
As designer Freddie Tavares remembered
twenty years later: "When we built the Stratocaster
we thought that it was the world's greatest guitar.
Then we said let's make something better, so we
built the Jazzmaster."
The body styling was clearly based on the Strat, although the
protruding "horns" on the upper bout were reduced considerably.
Intriguingly, the waist – the inward curves at each side of the body –
was offset. The most radical departure was in the sound: the wide
coils used in the pickups created a warmer, richer tone than
other Fender guitars. In spite of its name the
Jazzmaster still found wider favour
among pop players.

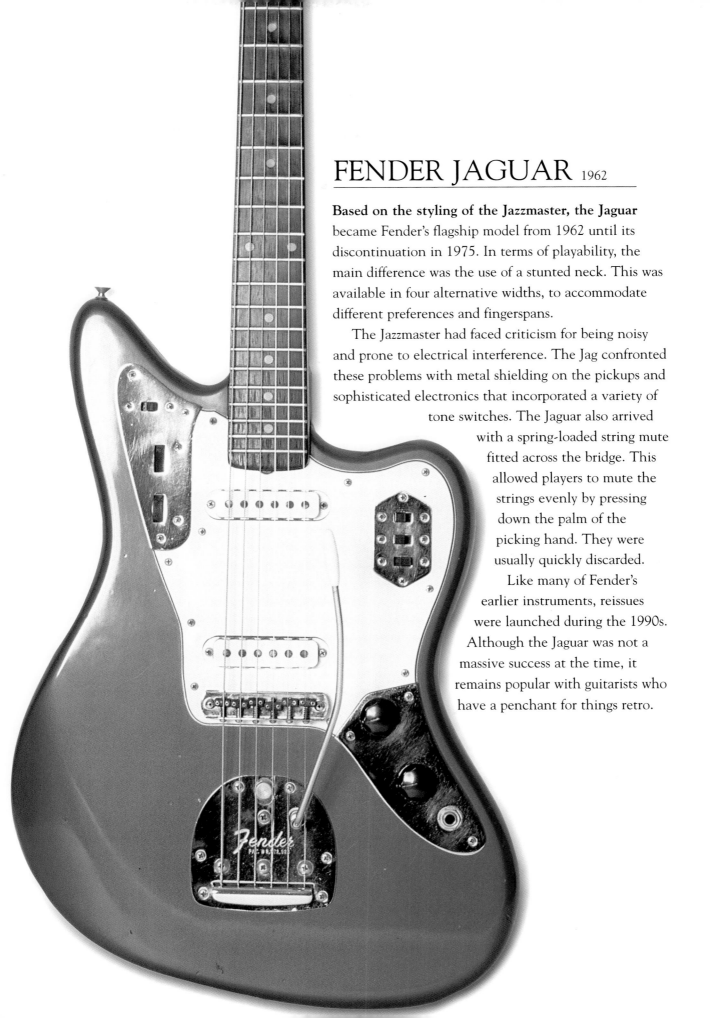

FENDER JAGUAR 1962

Based on the styling of the Jazzmaster, the Jaguar became Fender's flagship model from 1962 until its discontinuation in 1975. In terms of playability, the main difference was the use of a stunted neck. This was available in four alternative widths, to accommodate different preferences and fingerspans.

The Jazzmaster had faced criticism for being noisy and prone to electrical interference. The Jag confronted these problems with metal shielding on the pickups and sophisticated electronics that incorporated a variety of tone switches. The Jaguar also arrived with a spring-loaded string mute fitted across the bridge. This allowed players to mute the strings evenly by pressing down the palm of the picking hand. They were usually quickly discarded.

Like many of Fender's earlier instruments, reissues were launched during the 1990s. Although the Jaguar was not a massive success at the time, it remains popular with guitarists who have a penchant for things retro.

FENDER ELECTRIC XII 1965

The electric 12-string guitar became instantly fashionable in 1964, as guitarists marvelled at George Harrison's opening chimes on the Beatles', "Hard Day's Night". Shortly afterwards, US electric folk band the Byrds, created a sensation with a sound that almost entirely revolved around the 12-string electric.

Although both bands used Rickenbacker guitars, every other guitar manufacturer attempted to jump on the bandwagon. Fender's own foray – the Electric XII – was based on the "offset waist" styling of the Jazzmaster. An elongated headstock following the line of the fingerboard ended in a distinctive curved tip which later became known as the "hockey stick". Production of the Electric XII continued until 1968.

FENDER
SWINGER 1965

In 1956, Fender introduced its first range of so-called "student" guitars: the one-pickup Musicmaster, and the twin-pickup Duo-Sonic. These were three-quarter size instruments, with short-scale necks, and were designed for beginners or players on a tight budget. They were priced accordingly – the cheaper Musicmaster being around half the price of a Strat.

Fender continued to adopt this approach with the Swinger. Initially known around the Fender factory as the Arrow, the unusual cutaway at the base of the lower bout, and the curious "lopped-off" headstock were simply a result of cutting down left-over parts from existing models.

The guitar was produced briefly during 1969, and although it is no better than other Fender budget models, its relative scarcity has made it an attractive collectors' piece.

FENDER KATANA 1986

There can be little doubt that this is the least orthodox guitar Fender have produced to date. The Katana came about following pressure from Fender dealers who were feeling the pinch of the prevailing trend for unusual shaped guitars. Marketing Director Dan Smith recalled: "To pacify dealers we needed something ... I sat down with an art program on the Macintosh and screwed around, said, 'yeah this is no uglier than anyone else's'."

Surprisingly, the end result belied its humble (some might even say half-hearted) origins. But however happy the dealers might have been, the punters gave the Katana a wide berth. It was withdrawn within the year.

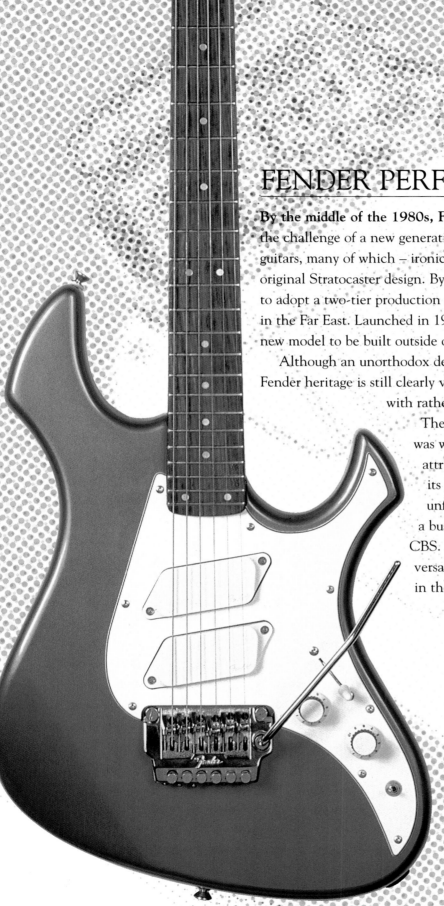

FENDER PERFORMER 1986

By the middle of the 1980s, Fender's traditional models faced the challenge of a new generation of high-performance rock guitars, many of which – ironically – were based around the original Stratocaster design. By this time, Fender had also begun to adopt a two-tier production system, producing cheaper models in the Far East. Launched in 1986, the Performer was the first new model to be built outside of the US.

Although an unorthodox design by their standards, the Fender heritage is still clearly visible – it appears to be a Swinger with rather angular horns.

The failure of the Performer – it was withdrawn in 1986 – can partly be attributed to "sniffy" attitudes toward its Japanese origins. It was also unfortunate to have appeared during a business crisis at parent company CBS. However, its reputation as a fine, versatile rock guitar has gradually risen in the years since its passing.

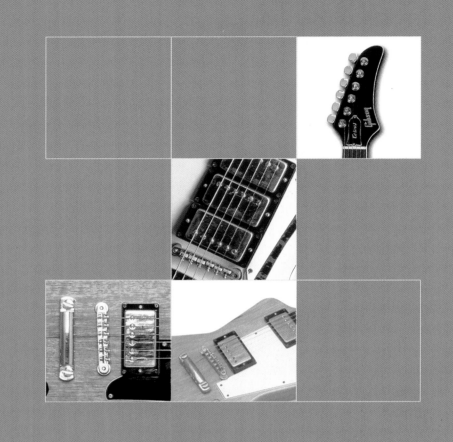

5
GIBSONS

SINCE ITS FOUNDATION IN THE NINETEENTH CENTURY, THE GIBSON NAME
HAS BEEN SYNONYMOUS WITH QUALITY. IN 1952, THE COMPANY RESPONSIBLE
FOR SOME OF THE MOST IMPORTANT INNOVATIONS IN THE GUITAR'S RECENT
HISTORY, LAUNCHED THE LEGENDARY "LES PAUL" – THE FIRST IN A LINE
OF MODELS THAT ALTHOUGH SLOW TO CATCH ON WITH MUSICIANS,
WERE SOON ACKNOWLEDGED AS DESIGN CLASSICS.

Gibson
Les Paul
Gibson
Les Paul
Gibson
Les Paul
Gibson
Les Paul

By the early 1950s, it became
clear that Gibson was in danger of losing its
coveted position as the world's most significant   guitar
manufacturer. Only a few years earlier, country player Les Paul had
brought his prototype "Log" guitar to the company headquarters in
Kalamazoo. As certain as he was that the next stage of the instrument's
development would be the use of a high-density body crafted from solid wood, Gibson's
decision makers were unimpressed. At the time they laughed at "the kid with the broomstick
guitar", but the success of Leo Fender's first production-line solid-body models now gave his
prophesy some credibility.

In 1951, Les Paul was invited to collaborate on the design for a solid-body instrument. The brief was simple:
the guitar would combine innovative design with the high production values for which Gibson was famed. Above

GIBSON LES PAUL MODEL ("GOLDTOP") 1952

all, it would provide serious competition to Fender's upstart designs. A year later, the first Gibson Les Paul
Model rolled off the assembly line. With its brightly-coloured finish, it soon became known as the "Goldtop".
Although guitar folklore may suggest otherwise, Les Paul's role in the design process was ultimately
limited to the electronics and the tailpiece mechanism. The body and headstock design were evidently
closely modelled on the smooth curves of Gibson's ES295 electric acoustic .

It's odd to think that an instrument now imbued with such iconic status should initially
have been so unsuccessful. One reason was cost: compared to the no-frills pragmatism of
Fender guitars, the Les Paul was more obviously a work of fine craftsmanship, but that
came at a price. The body was cut from natural mahogany with a carved maple
top. The neck was fixed to the body with glue, providing (in theory, at
least) greater sustain than Fender's less fancy bolt-on jobs. A 22-fret
rosewood fingerboard featured ornate mother-of-pearl
fingerboard inlays. This was without doubt a
luxury instrument.

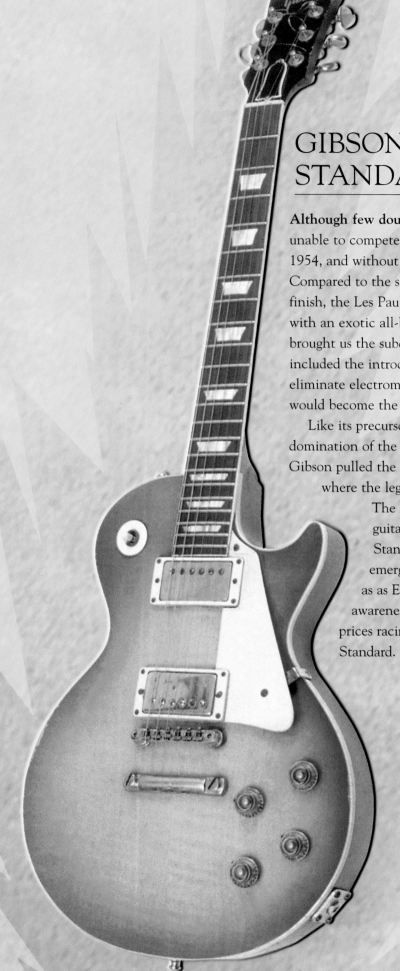

GIBSON LES PAUL STANDARD 1958

Although few doubted the qualities of the Les Paul Goldtop, it was unable to compete with the mighty Fender Stratocaster – launched in 1954, and without doubt the most famous guitar ever made. Compared to the subtle hues of the Strat's three-tone "sunburst" finish, the Les Paul seemed rather garish. Having experimented briefly with an exotic all-black Custom in 1954, four years later Gibson brought us the subdued tones of the Les Paul "Standard". Refinements included the introduction of the humbucking pickup: designed to eliminate electromagnetic hum, this was the final component in what would become the definitive Les Paul sound.

Like its precursor, the Standard was unable to stem Fender's domination of the electric guitar market, and barely two years later, Gibson pulled the plug on the Les Paul. Surprisingly, however, this is where the legend really starts.

The mid-1960s saw the emergence of a wave of young guitarists who found the combination of a Les Paul Standard and Marshall amplification unbeatable for the emerging blues-based rock sound. Influential names such as as Eric Clapton and Jimmy Page created a powerful awareness for this extinct model. In 1968, with secondhand prices racing ahead of demand, Gibson re-launched the Standard. It has remained in production ever since.

GIBSON ES355 1959

With a heritage built on the quality of their hollow-body guitars, in 1958, Gibson introduced a new series of instruments directed as much toward the rock 'n' roll player as their traditional jazz market. Spearheaded by the ES335, the elegant symmetrical design featured twin cutaways allowing more comfortable access to the top of the fingerboard. Launched the following year, the ES355 was essentially a "luxury" version of what has since become a classic instrument.

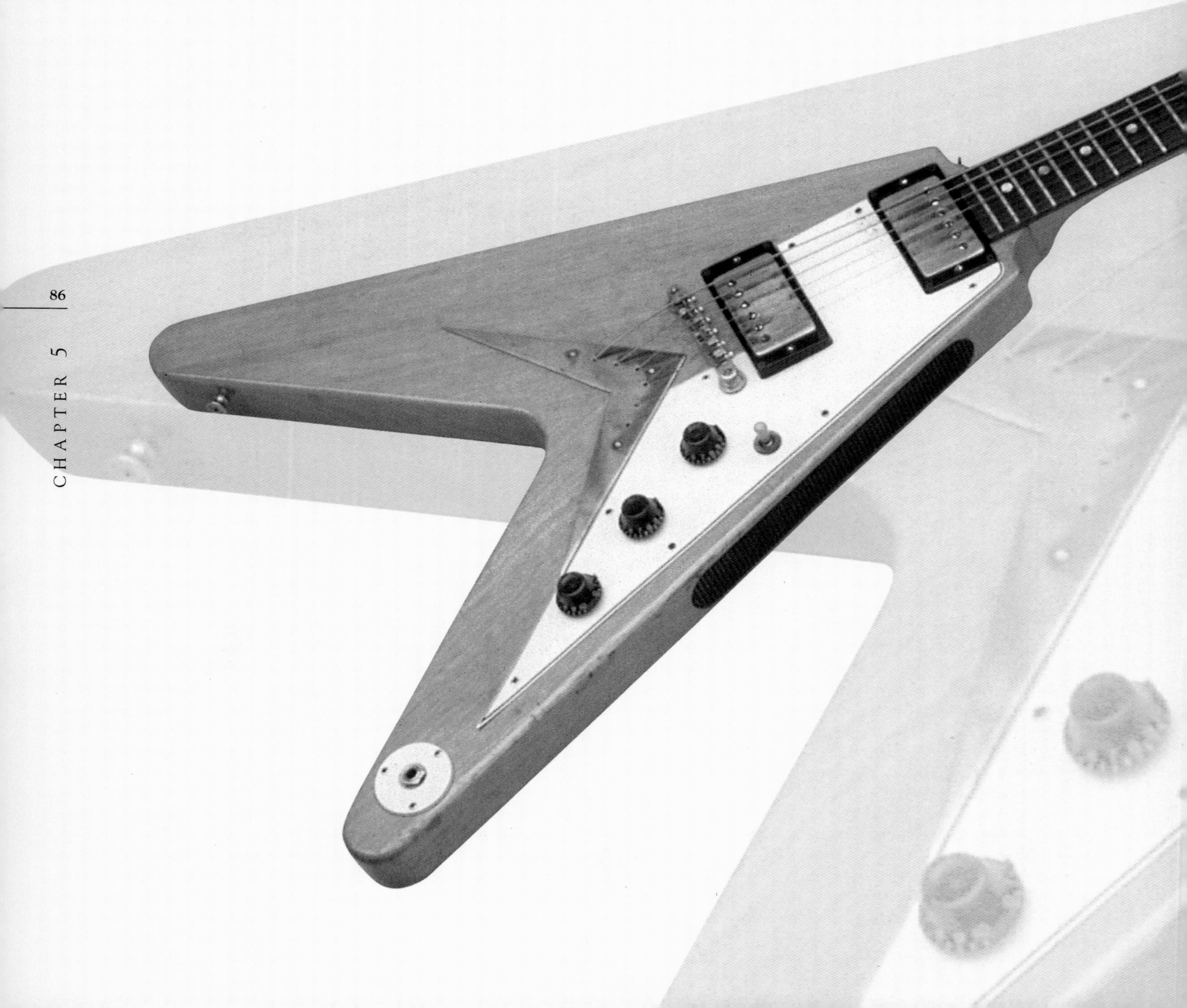

GIBSON FLYING V 1958

By the middle of the 1950s, a pattern of dominance had emerged in the market for solid-body electric guitars. The two major rivals vying for supremacy were Gibson and Fender. It was a battle of the old established giant versus the young upstart; less than a decade old and already a world-beater. As Gibson's president of the time, Ted McCarty, remembered: "Leo [Fender] was going around telling people that Gibson was stodgy and never had a new idea… and that Fender were the guitar company of the future."

Struggling to match Fender's success, in 1957 McCarty set a new goal: "To prove that Gibson was more modern than the rest." He looked at developments in other areas of American life, and in particular the angular shapes being used by the car designers of the era. In 1958, the first of Gibson's "new" instruments appeared: the Flying V. Previously, designs for solid-body electric guitars had been based largely around the curves of the traditional acoustic guitar; the Flying V, however,

took its cue from the lines of the triangular tailfins that featured on many of the mighty American automobiles of the decade.

The Flying V wasn't the most practical instrument: since the body made no reference to the standard figure-of-eight guitar shape, there was no way it could be played in a sitting position. No, it was aimed squarely at the stage performer, and since, by comparison, it rendered every other instrument conservative in the extreme, we can assume that Gibson had the more extrovert musician in mind.

It may have been a revolutionary instrument, but the Flying V bombed spectacularly. Only about eighty originals were produced, and the line was dropped in 1959. Like the Les Paul, it later found favour among a number of rock players, prompting Gibson to produce a modified version in 1966. Authenticated originals now change hands for hefty sums of money.

GIBSON
EXPLORER 1958

Conceived and created in 1958 at the same time as the Flying V, the Gibson Explorer was every bit as radical a design as its more lauded partner. But it was no more successful: again only around eighty original models were built before production ended in 1959. Like the Flying V, the Explorer departed from Gibson's traditional materials, cutting the bodies from African korina (limba) wood rather than natural mahogany. Although the woods are similar in appearance and density, korina is much lighter than mahogany: the weight of the original Les Paul models was often cited as a reason for their initial unpopularity – even though it was a contributing factor to their unique sound.

The distinguishing feature of the Explorer was its unique "back-to-front" styling. Other electric guitars were visually more balanced, normally constructed with a cutaway beneath the neck joint – countered above the neck by an overhanging upper bout. By contrast, the Explorer extended the upper bout beneath the neck to a sharp point; the bout above the neck was almost non-existent. The Explorer was also Gibson's first guitar to feature the Fender-style slanted headstock with all six machine heads running along the same edge.

Less futuristic than the Flying V – and arguably more practical – the Explorer body style would later emerge in a modified form in the Gibson Firebird guitar and electric bass models.

GIBSON MODERNE 1958

The Moderne was the third design in Gibson's futuristic revamp of 1958. But unlike the Flying V, on which the top half of the body is clearly styled, the Moderne didn't even make it to the production line at that time. It was a growing interest in original models that prompted Gibson to launch a reissue model in 1983.

GIBSON SG 1961

The early 1960s saw Gibson still
struggling with the phenomenal growth of the solid-body
electric guitar market. The Les Paul Standard in its original form had been
taken off the production line to be replaced, in 1961, by the new Les Paul Standard
– a modern-looking instrument that Gibson hoped would capture the imagination of young,
image-conscious players.

Although the two instruments were similar in most respects, the body shape represented
something of a departure. Whereas the "old" Les Paul featured a small upper bout with a single
cutaway, the new version styled both upper and lower bouts in broadly similar proportions, creating
an almost traditional figure-of-eight effect. The heavily bevelled twin cutaways were designed to
give the player unprecedented access to the top of the fingerboard.

Despite the fact that the instrument was initially launched as the next incarnation of the
Standard, Les Paul himself didn't like the new body shape and requested that his famed
signature be removed from the headstock. So, from 1962, the guitar became known as the
Gibson SG – "Solid Guitar".

Like the many reissues of the Les Paul over the fifty years following its launch,
a number of variations on the original SG design have appeared. The version
shown here is an early-1960s SG custom featuring three
humbucking pickups.

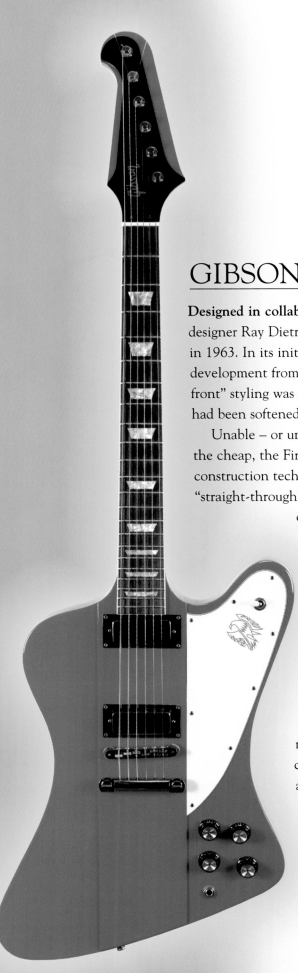

GIBSON FIREBIRD 1963

Designed in collaboration with American automobile designer Ray Dietrich, the Gibson Firebird first appeared in 1963. In its initial form, the Firebird could be seen as a development from the ill-fated Explorer. The "back-to-front" styling was still there, but the sharp, angular look had been softened with gentle, flowing curves.

Unable – or unprepared – to produce instruments on the cheap, the Firebird took Gibson's previous solid-body construction techniques one stage further by creating a "straight-through" neck. In other words, the neck and central body panel – the area holding the bridge, vibrato tailpiece and humbucking pickups – was carved from a solid piece of wood. The "wings" above and below were glued separately.

Expensive, and not that popular, in 1965 the Firebird was overhauled. The less expensive glued neck system used on Les Pauls and SGs was introduced, and the body styling was radically altered.

To all intents and purposes the original models (such as the one shown here) are completely different guitars and are known as "Reverse" Firebirds; the later models, "Non-reverse" Firebirds.

GIBSON
DOUBLE 12 1962

Although luthiers had experimented by
making instruments with multiple necks before the guitar
had even been amplified, it wasn't until electrification that the idea
began to capture the imagination of the working musician. The logic was
simple: it provided the live performer with a means of making an instant
changeover between different sounding instruments. Although models
comprising electric bass and six-string guitar have been produced (or even
two bass guitars, as fans of Spinal Tap will attest), the most versatile
combination is of six and twelve strings.

It was in the late 1950s that the first Gibson Double 12 guitars
appeared. Not intended as production-line models, they were built
to order. Players not requiring a twelve-string neck also had the
option of the Double Mandolin – a similar instrument that
twinned six-string and mandolin necks.

In 1962, Gibson launched its
production line "second series"
twin necks, with body styling
based on the contours of
the newly launched
Gibson SG.

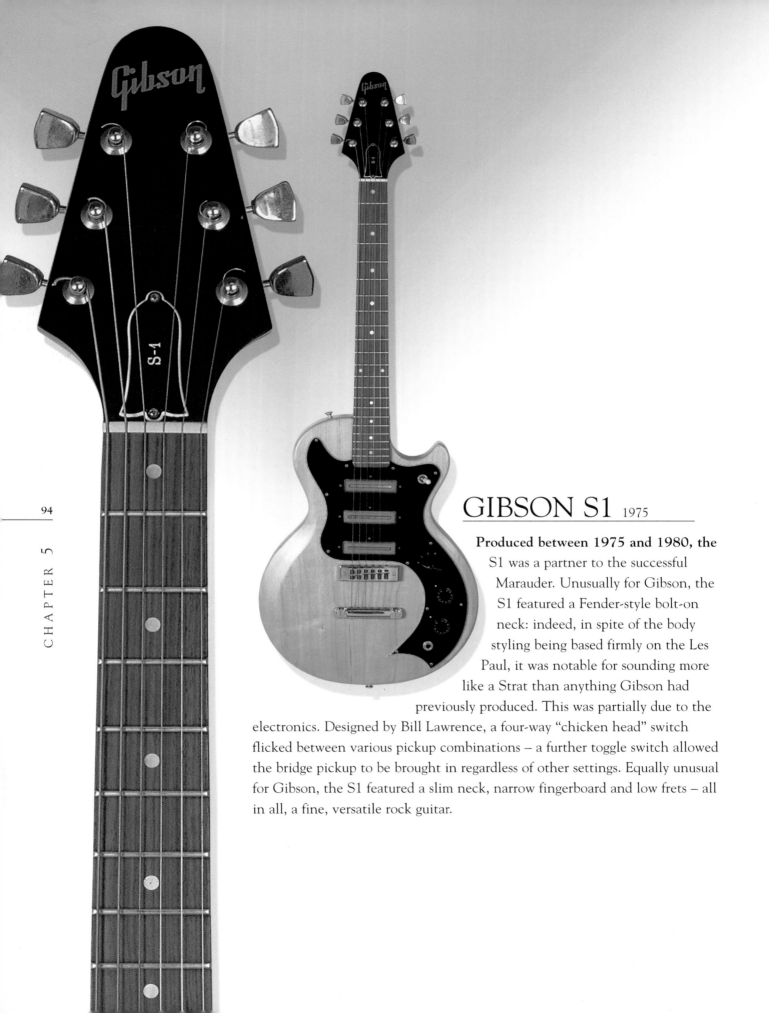

GIBSON S1 1975

Produced between 1975 and 1980, the S1 was a partner to the successful Marauder. Unusually for Gibson, the S1 featured a Fender-style bolt-on neck: indeed, in spite of the body styling being based firmly on the Les Paul, it was notable for sounding more like a Strat than anything Gibson had previously produced. This was partially due to the electronics. Designed by Bill Lawrence, a four-way "chicken head" switch flicked between various pickup combinations – a further toggle switch allowed the bridge pickup to be brought in regardless of other settings. Equally unusual for Gibson, the S1 featured a slim neck, narrow fingerboard and low frets – all in all, a fine, versatile rock guitar.

GIBSON CORVUS III 1983

By the start of the 1980s, the concept of the "vintage" guitar was well established. The Gibson Les Paul and SG models were by now widely viewed as classic instruments, with re-issues and variations providing the company with the bulk of its income. The perceived desirability of these guitars was further fuelled by a vibrant and well-publicised secondhand market for original models from the 1950s, which could now be seen changing hands for the price of a new car.

However, the prevailing fashion at the cutting edge of guitar manufacture was for the Fender-inspired "Superstrat" guitars, and once again, Gibson felt compelled to come up with something new. One response was this 1983 Gibson Corvus III. A candidate for one of the least popular instruments Gibson ever produced, it certainly rates as a design curiosity. Looking more than a little like a giant bottle opener, the Corvus also bore a superficial resemblance to the Ovation solid-body instruments of the late-1970s. It came in three variations, the I, II and III – the numeral denoting the number of pickups. The most commonly produced colours were silver and this vibrant orange.

Of course, as a Gibson production model, the Corvus was an extremely playable instrument, but it sold in very small quantities. Within a couple of years the Corvus was a distant memory, and Gibson once again concentrated on its core classics.

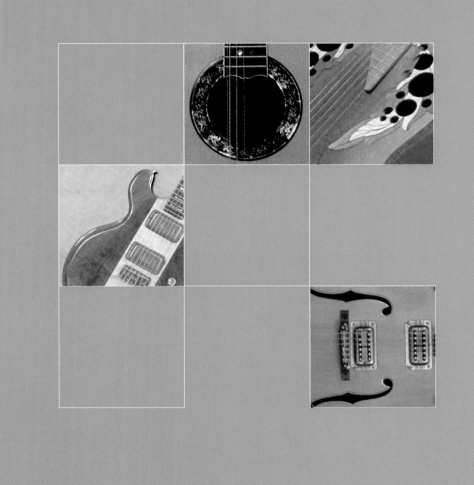

6
OTHER US CLASSICS

ALTHOUGH FENDER AND GIBSON ARE THE TWO BEST-KNOWN NAMES IN THE STORY OF THE ELECTRIC GUITAR, MANY OTHER COMPANIES – SOME WITH NOTABLE HERITAGES OF THEIR OWN – HAVE MADE THEIR MARK IN THIS FIELD. RICKENBACKER, EPIPHONE, GRETSCH AND OVATION, TO NAME BUT A FEW, HAVE ALL PRODUCED IMPORTANT AND INNOVATIVE MODELS THAT HAVE STOOD THE TEST OF TIME.

GRETSCH 6120 CHET ATKINS 1954

The guitars produced during the 1950s by the Fred Gretsch company are the very embodiment of the art of the guitar. Whilst Fender aimed for production-line simplicity, and Gibson upheld their traditional high production values, the Gretsch boast was that their guitars were prettier than the rest!

Launched in 1954, the Gretsch 6120 was a collaboration with Country's greatest picker, Chet Atkins. A hollow-body model, the 6120 was styled in a glowing orange "Amber Red". As a testament to its Country roots, the original models featured a "G" branded on the body, a longhorn motif at the top of the headstock and a variety of cactus images on the fingerboard inlays – like those shown on the 6130 Round Up across the page.

As with other Gretsch guitars, the 6120 was a delicate creature – extremely light, with a body made from thin laminated maple. Nor was it a masterpiece of practical design: the bridge was not attached to the body, but held in place by string tension, making it easy to knock out of position if light strings were used; furthermore, it was only possible to alter the overall height of the bridge, not the individual strings. The guitar also featured the famously chunky Bigsby Patent vibrato arm, which, if over-used, could send the instrument out of tune. It was the DeArmond pickups that gave the 6120 its fabulously distinctive sound – one that would make it a favourite among 1950s rockabilly players like Eddie Cochran and Duane Eddy. Later 6120s (as shown on the 1958 model above) used the improved Filtertron humbucking pickup.

A frequent criticism of Gretsches was that no two examples of the same model ever sounded the same. But when a guitar looks as good as this, who could really care less?

GRETSCH
6130 ROUND UP 1954

Introduced in 1954, the 6130 Round Up featured much of the same Western-inspired styling as the 6120. In fact, it was closely modelled on the 6121 Chet Atkins solid body guitar, only with a " knotty pine" top (instead of maple), and the cowboy "belt buckle" tailpiece replacing the Bigsby vibrato arm. The body styling – like the 6121 – was based around the contours of the Gibson Les Paul.

Although Gretsch produced many other solid-body instruments, it is for their semi-solid and hollow-body 1950s classics that the name is so revered.

GRETSCH 6136
WHITE FALCON 1954

When the prototype model of the Gretsch White Falcon was first
displayed in public at a 1954 musical instruments trade fair in Chicago, it
was billed as "The Guitar of the Future". It might not exactly have provided
a template for instruments that followed, but is unquestionably one of the
most distinctive and stylish guitars ever to the come off a production line.

Designed by demonstrator Jimmie Webster, the hollow-body White
Falcon was Gretsch's flagship guitar until production ceased in 1980.
Stunning in its gleaming white finish, the Falcon appeared even more
opulent with its gold-plated hardware and "Gold Sparkle" binding. White
Falcons were produced with a single-cutaway body until 1963, when double
cutaways became standard.

The Gretsch company – seemingly like most of the other great
American musical instrument pioneers – was started up by an enterprising
European immigrant, Friedrich Gretsch, who in 1893 opened his first music
store in New York. However, it was not until the 1930s that his son Fred
would preside over the manufacture of the first Gretsch guitars. What could
be termed the classic Gretsch era came to an end in 1967 when the
company – which was equally famed for its drums and percussion – was
swallowed up by the Baldwin musical instrument group. Production of
Gretsch guitars continued until 1981.

By the end of the 1980s, ownership of the name and various patents
returned to the Gretsch family, who resumed production of some of their
classic 1950s models – this time in Japan. Although the new guitars may
have lost some of their individual quirks, it's probably fair to say that in
many cases they are consistently "better" instruments than the originals.

GRETSCH 6134
WHITE PENGUIN 1954

The 6134 White Penguin could be seen as the solid-body partner
to the White Falcon. It is essentially a restyled version of the 6128 DuoJet,
launched earlier in 1954 to compete directly with the Gibson Les Paul.
Shown here is a highly collectible 1961 model with a
symmetrical double cutaway – a feature only found on models
made between 1961 and their discontinuation three years later.

GRETSCH 6129
SILVERJET 1954

1954 was clearly a big year for Gretsch. As well as many of their other
classic models, the company also launched a series of three
"Jet" models: the 6128 DuoJet; the 6129 SilverJet; and
6131 Jet Firebird. With the exception of their body
colour (black, silver and red, respectively), the three
guitars were identical.

The SilverJet appears in the same Silver Sparkle finish
used on many Gretsch drum kits. The SilverJet remained
in production until 1963.

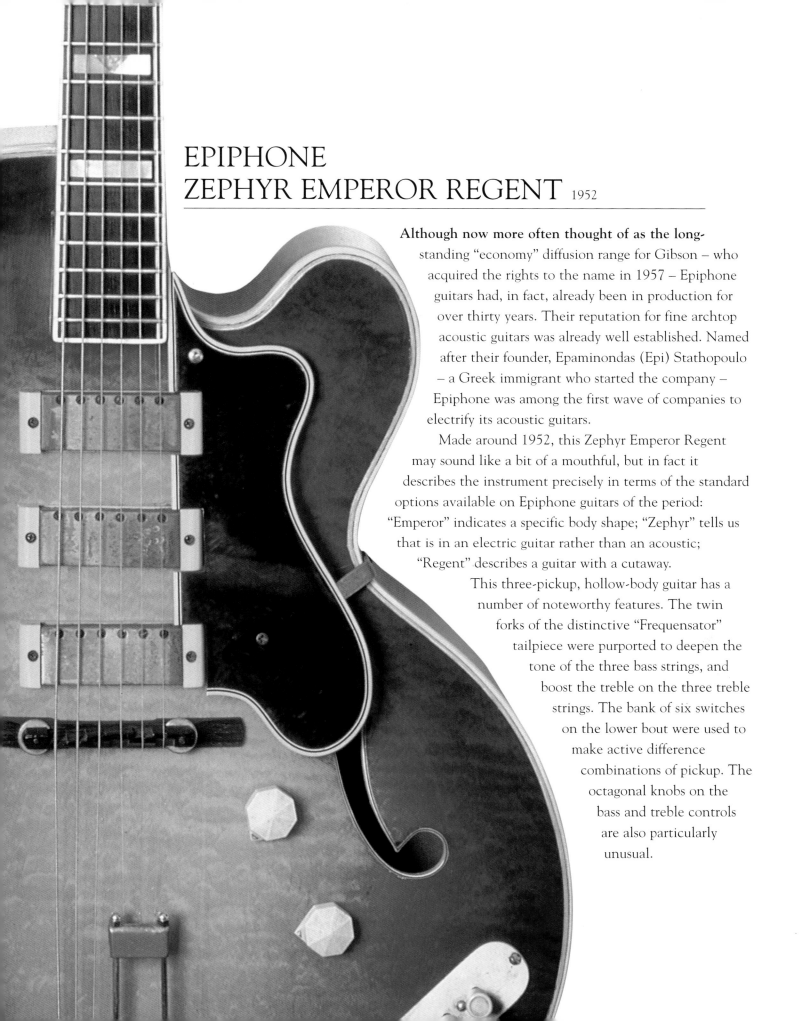

EPIPHONE
ZEPHYR EMPEROR REGENT 1952

Although now more often thought of as the long-
standing "economy" diffusion range for Gibson – who
acquired the rights to the name in 1957 – Epiphone
guitars had, in fact, already been in production for
over thirty years. Their reputation for fine archtop
acoustic guitars was already well established. Named
after their founder, Epaminondas (Epi) Stathopoulo
– a Greek immigrant who started the company –
Epiphone was among the first wave of companies to
electrify its acoustic guitars.

Made around 1952, this Zephyr Emperor Regent
may sound like a bit of a mouthful, but in fact it
describes the instrument precisely in terms of the standard
options available on Epiphone guitars of the period:
"Emperor" indicates a specific body shape; "Zephyr" tells us
that is in an electric guitar rather than an acoustic;
"Regent" describes a guitar with a cutaway.

This three-pickup, hollow-body guitar has a
number of noteworthy features. The twin
forks of the distinctive "Frequensator"
tailpiece were purported to deepen the
tone of the three bass strings, and
boost the treble on the three treble
strings. The bank of six switches
on the lower bout were used to
make active difference
combinations of pickup. The
octagonal knobs on the
bass and treble controls
are also particularly
unusual.

EPIPHONE PROFESSIONAL 1963

Like the Zephyr Emperor, the Epiphone Professional also features some unusual electronic styling. Most of the controls on the bass-side of this unusual thinline, archtop hollow body were designed to work in conjunction with the instrument's own special amplifier. Among the possibilities were tone boosts, reverb and tremolo effects, all of which were set up on the amp, but could be switched in and out from the body of the guitar.

Not a particularly great instrument in its own right, and with the added expense of a specific amplifier, the Professional failed to capture the imagination of the guitar-playing masses and was discontinued in 1967.

RICKENBACKER 360-12 1964

As one of the most significant pioneering names in the story of the electric guitar, the Rickenbacker company enjoyed a surprisingly low profile during the 1940s. In 1953 the company was sold to American businessman, Charles C. Hall. Under his guidance, the Rickenbacker name enjoyed a considerable revival, producing some of the most fashionable instruments of the 1960s.

From their inception in 1958, the sweeping lines of the Rickenbacker hollow-body six-string electrics were more than capable of turning heads. There were certainly no other electric acoustic instruments quite like them, the distinctive "slash" soundhole a dramatic contrast to the usual double "f" holes more commonly found.

Rickenbacker guitars became massively popular in 1963 when John Lennon and George Harrison were seen playing short-scale 325 guitars on stage. During the Beatles' 1964 US tour, George Harrison was presented with one of the first 360-12s: one its first uses can be heard on the opening "E seventh suspended" chord that

heralds the opening of the classic single, "A Hard Days Night". Patronage followed by the revered US country-rock band the Byrds, whose sound all but revolved around the jangling 360-12.

A unique features of the 360-12 were the headstock designs and machine head mechanisms. Whereas other 12-string makers produced ugly elongated headstocks large enough to accommodate the additional six machine heads, Rickenbacker devised a cunning system, mounting the extra six heads in classical-style slots between and perpendicular to the others. Although they could be fiddly to use they nonetheless gave an overall sense of balance to the guitar.

Although by no means the original twelve-string electric guitar, the Rickenbacker 360-12 was certainly the first to become fashionable. Its importance to the sound of some of the most enduring mid-1960s pop music ensures its place in guitar history.

RICKENBACKER 381 1958

Using the classic Rickenbacker hollow-body shape, the 381 was one of the less common arch-top, thick-bodied models.

Among the other unusual design features common to Rickenbackers of the period is the two-piece split-level scratch plate, housing a pickup selector switch, with individual tone and volume controls for each pickup. The smaller of the five knobs is a "mix" control, which allows the player to alter the balance between the lead and rhythm pickups.

The 381 was manufactured between 1958 and 1963, and again between 1969 and 1974.

RICKENBACKER
"LIGHT SHOW" 331 1970

In 1970, Rickenbacker gave us this fascinating exhibit. Based on a standard 330 model, the "Light Show" featured a hollowed out body with a clear perspex top. Coloured light bulbs were fitted inside which flickered depending on the frequency of the notes being played. The effect was created via connection to an external flashing unit. Since the visual effect was always dependant on the string being struck, the light patterns were always in perfect time with the music.

An unusual instrument that perhaps reflects the era in which it appeared, small numbers of the 331 were produced until 1975.

DANELECTRO
4123 GUITARLIN 1959

After spending many years building amplifiers for Epiphone, in 1947 Nate Daniel started the New Jersey-based Danelectro company. Successfully continuing in the same line of business, by 1948 Daniel had become the exclusive guitar amplifier producer for Sears & Roebuck. In 1954, he was asked by Sears to produce a range of economy solid-body electric guitars. Appearing under the Silvertone brand, these early models were constructed of cheap solid poplar wood, their bodies covered in a mauve-coloured vinyl. At the same time, Daniel began to sell similar instruments to different stores using the Danelectro name.

From 1956, Daniel started to produce Danelectro guitars using even cheaper materials and construction. On new models, pieces of poplar wood were stapled together to create a frame, comprising the sides, neck and bridge block. They were then covered in thick "masonite" – or hardboard. The tops and backs were painted, and the bare sides covered in vinyl.

Danelectro guitars were not particularly renowned for either their sound or playability. These were budget models that initially sold for under $40 – less than a quarter of the price of a nice Gibson. One thing's for sure though – what they may have lacked in finesse was more than made up for in visual distinctiveness.

One of the most unusual Danelectro models was the Guitarlin. The heavily scooped double cutaway "Longhorn" body gave an unprecedented access to a 31-fret fingerboard – over two-and-a-half octaves. The instrument takes its name from combining a "guitar" with a "mandolin". Access to the unusually high notes was provided to mimic the range of the mandolin either when playing barre chords or using a capo device. On a practical level, this was not quite as useful as it might have seemed, not least because the cheap materials used ensured very poor levels of sustain in the upper register. It does look *very* cool, though.

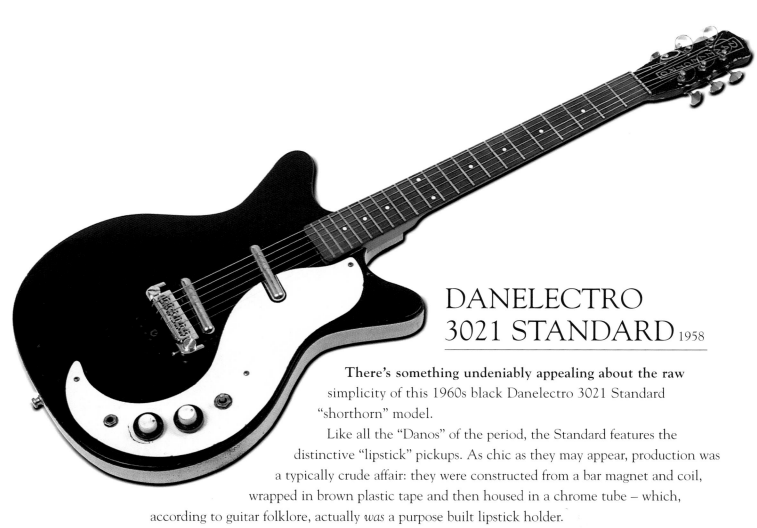

DANELECTRO
3021 STANDARD 1958

There's something undeniably appealing about the raw
simplicity of this 1960s black Danelectro 3021 Standard
"shorthorn" model.

Like all the "Danos" of the period, the Standard features the
distinctive "lipstick" pickups. As chic as they may appear, production was
a typically crude affair: they were constructed from a bar magnet and coil,
wrapped in brown plastic tape and then housed in a chrome tube – which,
according to guitar folklore, actually *was* a purpose built lipstick holder.

Yet in spite of the myriad shortcomings, no less a figure than Jimmy Page could be seen
using a 3021 on stage with Led Zeppelin during the 1970s. And even Eric Clapton had a
customised "psychedelic" shorthorn that he used with Cream.

DANELECTRO 3923
DOUBLE NECK 1959

Although twin neck guitars are more normally six- and twelve-string affairs, this shorthorn, single-pickup "Stan and Dan" model combines a Standard six-string guitar with a bass guitar. It was – according to the Danelectro sales catalogue of the time – the only twin-neck the company produced.

Danelectro continued to produce guitars until 1969 when the company went out of business. In the late 1990s, the US Evets Corporation bought the name, and began producing a new line of reissues. The modern instruments have the advantage of combining classic retro looks with contemporary construction methods. Although the guitars are cheaply built in Korea, they are set up in the US before they hit the stores.

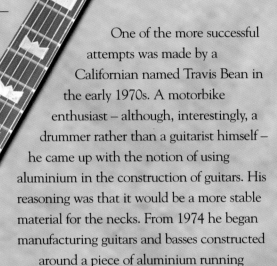

KRAMER 450 1977

Although wood has invariably been the standard material used in the construction of musical instruments, many guitar makers have experimented with alternatives. It's fair to say that few have made much of an impact.

One of the more successful attempts was made by a Californian named Travis Bean in the early 1970s. A motorbike enthusiast – although, interestingly, a drummer rather than a guitarist himself – he came up with the notion of using aluminium in the construction of guitars. His reasoning was that it would be a more stable material for the necks. From 1974 he began manufacturing guitars and basses constructed around a piece of aluminium running from the neck through to the bridge. His aim was to improve the sound and sustain of the guitar. Despite some high-profile admirers, however, the idea, failed to catch on, and production ceased in 1979.

A few years earlier, in 1976, one of Bean's salesmen, Gary Kramer, launched his own guitar company. Kramer guitars were very similar in appearance to Travis Beans – even down to the unusual materials used. The principal difference was that the Kramer aluminium neck was bolted on to a conventional wooden body. Kramer guitars certainly made an impact, but remained a cult interest. By 1985, Kramer had phased out aluminum altogether, and for a while successfully manufactured "Superstrat" style rock guitars.

KRAMER SUSTAINER 1989

Realising that concentrating their efforts on aluminium-necked instruments was always going to render them a specialist company, in the early 1980s Kramer focussed their efforts on the burgeoning "metal" market. Working with finger-tapping supremo Eddie Van Halen and a young New Zealander named Floyd Rose, Kramer was instrumental in bringing the locking tremolo arm to the market. With the strings clamped at both the nut and the bridge, it became possible to create "dive-bomber" pitch-bending effects and bring the instrument back to perfect tune. The Floyd Rose locking tremolo system became industry standard almost overnight.

In 1989, Kramer and Floyd Rose came up with another impressive – but rather less significant – innovation, the Sustainer. On the surface, it appears to be a fairly standard rock guitar, with Stratocaster styling, upward-pointing headstock and twin humbucking pickups. The clever part was in the neck-position pickup. At the flick of a switch, it would generate a battery-powered electro-magnetic effect which would cause already vibrating strings to sustain indefinitely.

By this time, however, Kramer was running into business difficulties and the following year he went into liquidation. In 1996, the company was acquired by Gibson.

OVATION CUSTOM LEGEND 1976

The American Ovation company was arguably the most important manufacturer of acoustic guitars to emerge during the twentieth century. It was founded in 1966 by wealthy industrialist Charles Kaman, an engineer who had made his fortune designing and manufacturing helicopter blades.

Ovation's most radical innovation was the complete overhaul of the traditional acoustic guitar body. The back and sides were replaced by a one-piece "bowl", crafted from a newly developed fibreglass resin that the company dubbed "Lyrachord". With no joins or body strutting needed to support the top of the guitar, the sound could no longer be trapped in the corners of the soundbox. This created a purer tone and enabled greater volume. The first Ovation guitar to be launched in this style was the 1966 Balladeer. In 1970, this was also made available as an electro-acoustic instrument. It was here that the company would find their greatest success.

Traditionally, the close-miking of acoustic guitars on stage posed logistical problems for sound engineers: the volume and tone could vary, or sounds could "spill" from other louder instruments. Ovation's solution was to create a unique electro-acoustic instrument with piezo electric transducer pickups positioned beneath each string on the underside of the bridge saddle.

The guitar shown here is a 1976 Custom Legend 12-string.

OVATION ADAMAS 1975

In 1975, Ovation launched the Adamas as their top-of-the-line model.
An extremely attractive and unorthodox electro-acoustic instrument,
the most most striking feature is the lack of a central sound hole.
Instead, the sound is dispersed through a series of different-sized
sound holes that appear in the upper bout on both sides of
the fingerboard. Unlike previous Ovations, the top of the
body is not made wholly from natural materials, but
from layers of carbon fibre and birch veneers.

During the 1990s, Ovation adopted the name
Adamas for its diffusion
range of economy
models.

OVATION BREADWINNER 1972

Having quickly established themselves as the most significant name in the field of electro-acoustic guitars, it was inevitable that Ovation should try their hand at a solid-body instrument. Their first attempt, launched in 1972, was the Breadwinner.

The most interesting design feature of the Breadwinner is the cutaway in the lower bout, which was intended to provide the guitar with a better balance when seated. However, the original designer later admitted that the inspiration for the shape came about because guitarists of the period often referred to their instruments as their "axe". It was also initially intended that the body be made out of the same Lyrachord resin used on Ovation's celebrated electric acoustics, but before

production this idea was abandoned in favour of solid mahogany. Other ideas floated at the time were to give the body a hollowed-out honeycomb structure, making the guitar lightweight but quite strong.

There was also a Breadwinner Limited model, which was the same basic shape, but featured a sculpted cutaway on the body above the pickups. The same shape was also used on the "deluxe" Deacon six- and twelve-string models.

Given the general conservatism of guitar players as a breed, the rather odd styling of the Breadwinner was inevitably going to limit sales. However, it possesses a "love-it-or-loathe-it" quality that has created a reputation for it as one of the cult guitars of the 1970s.

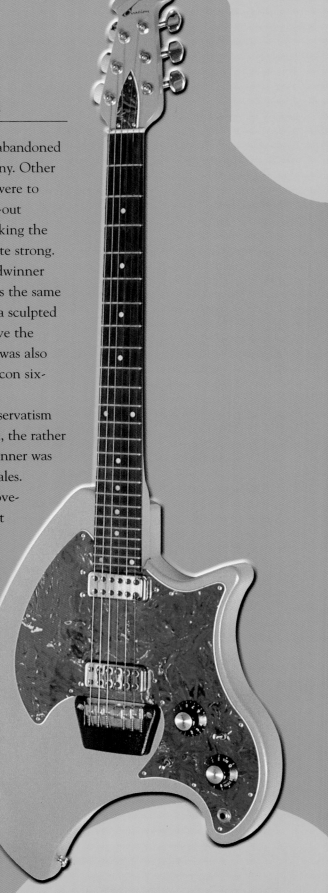

OVATION VIPER 1975

After blazing the trail with the Breadwinner, Ovation adopted a more conventional, approach for their next attempt at the solid-body market. The 1975 Viper came in a variety of beautiful finishes, had an excellent Strat-like sound, and – like all the other Ovation solids – featured a cutaway that gave access to the 24th fret.

Like the Ovation Preacher – launched at the same time – the Viper simply failed to capture the imagination of the 1970s guitarist. As such, production ceased in 1982, after which Ovation retired from the solid-body business, concentrating wholly on the electric acoustic instruments for which they became market leaders.

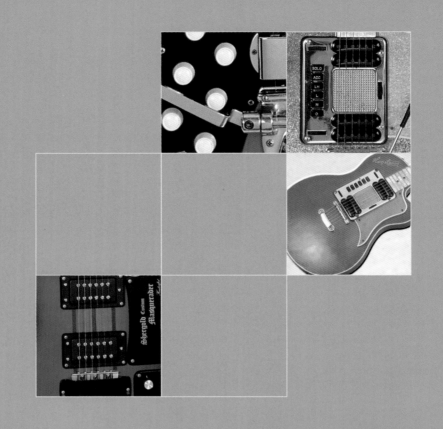

7
EUROPE/REST OF THE WORLD SOLIDS

ALTHOUGH THE GUITAR'S ORIGINS ARE EUROPEAN, MOST OF THE MAJOR RECENT DEVELOPMENTS HAVE TAKEN PLACE IN AMERICA. TRADE REGULATIONS MEANT THAT MANY OF THE GREAT ELECTRICS OF THE 1950s WERE RARELY SEEN OUTSIDE THE UNITED STATES. EUROPEAN AND JAPANESE GUITAR MAKERS CATERED FOR DEMAND BY MAKING INFERIOR DERIVATIVES – IN SOME CASES, WITH UNIQUE REGIONAL FLAIR.

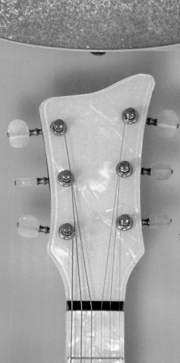

HAGSTROM
P46 1959

Before turning his attention to guitars, Albin Hagström had been one of Europe's biggest manufacturers of accordions. Sweden may never have been a hotbed of rock and roll action, nevertheless towards the end of the 1950s, Hagström noticed a growing demand for electric guitars.

Like Danelectro in the US, the Hagstrom company's primary aim was to find the most economic means of producing low-cost guitars. One of the first instruments off the production line was the P46 Deluxe, produced between 1958 and 1962. Like many guitars of the period, the body shape echoed the Gibson Les Paul, although the true inspiration was evidently German-built models by Framus and Hofner, whose success Hagstrom hoped to emulate.

The neck of the P46 Deluxe is unusual in that it features a plexiglass fretboard with stainless steel frets. And if the three pickups of a Fender Stratocaster weren't enough, this baby had four! Visually, the push-button control panel and "sparkle" finish look every bit as if they were originally intended for use on an accordion.

HAGSTROM KENT
BP24G 1962

The Hagstrom "Kent" – or model BP24G as it was known in the sales catalogue – was a blatant copy of a Fender Stratocaster – not only in body shape, but also in the curves of the headstock.

Cheap in every way, the Kent was firmly aimed at the beginner or casual player. The body was built from poplar and spruce plywood – of the type used to make loading pallets. To further reduce costs, the back of the body was covered in vinyl; the front top required no specialised finishing, being a piece of see-through plexiglass sprayed on the reverse side.

Like other Hagstroms, the Kent featured the Tremar vibrato arm. This was designed for gentle pitch variations of no more than a semitone – anything more wreaked havoc with the guitar's tuning.

Unique among manufacturers, Hagstrom instruments featured the brand logo on the upper bout of the body rather than on the more usual headstock: the cross on the letter "t" was extended to the end of the word to fudge the question of whether or not to place an umlaut over the letter "o".

Fascinatingly enough, this rather unprepossessing guitar enjoys a rather special accolade in that, even now, it remains the biggest-selling single European model ever made – with sales of over 25,000 between 1962 and 1967.

The final Hagstroms came off the production line in 1983. Pat Smear of the US rock band Foo Fighters – a huge fan – is purported to have tried unsuccessfully to buy the name with a view to resuscitating Hagstrom as a brand.

EKO 700/4V 1964

The Eko brand was founded in 1959 by Oliviero Pigini and Company of Recanati, Italy. As one might have expected, the first Italian takes on the electric guitar were not lacking in stylistic panache: indeed, many of the first guitars produced by Italian brands such as Eko, Bartolini and Crucianelli looked nothing like the guitars being produced in the rest of the world.

The Eko 700/4V was introduced as the company's flagship model in 1964. Although the tone buttons and "mother-of-toilet-seat" plastic finish wouldn't look out of place on an accordion, the Eko brand was exclusively concerned with producing guitars and basses.

With its four double-pole Alnico V pickups, this model is especially interesting because it features six tone buttons, each with suitably evocative names such as "Twang" and "Jazz".

The 700/4V must rate among the thinnest guitars ever produced, the body measuring barely one inch in depth.

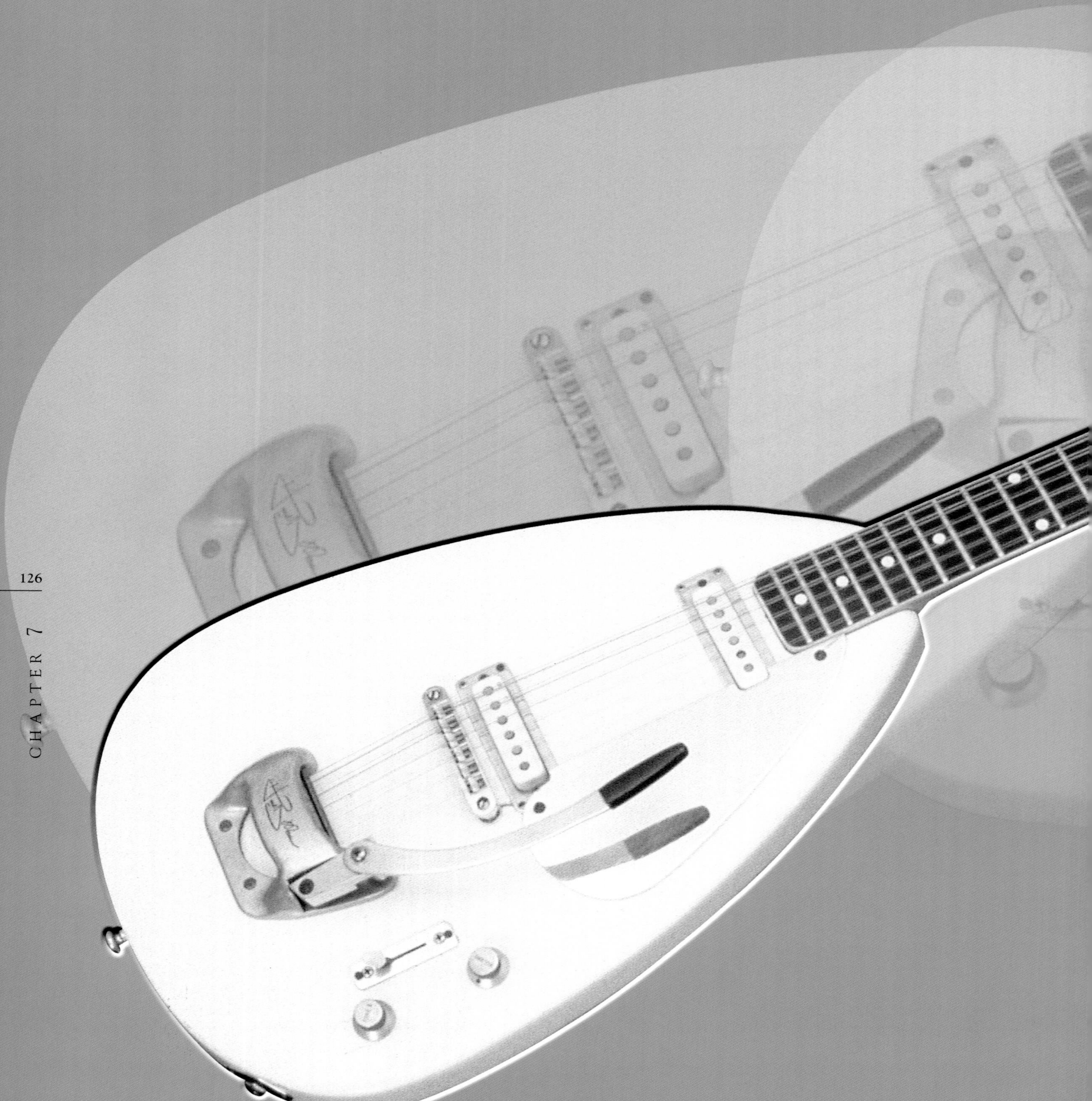

VOX "TEARDROP" XII 1967

In 1958, London-based Jennings Musical Instruments launched the Vox AC15 guitar amplifier, followed some two years later by the now-legendary AC30. The first prominent users of Vox equipment were the Shadows. One of Britain's most popular groups at that time, they were almost single-handedly responsible for popularising the Vox brand name.

The first guitars to bear the Vox brand were from a rather non-descript range of Italian imports. In 1961, with the popularity of the electric guitar soaring, Jennings decided to introduce his own British-manufactured model.

"A New Sound with a Different Shape" was the rather prosaic pronouncement from Vox when the unusual coffin-shaped Phantoms were first advertised. With its striking offset trapezoid body, the Phantom was one of the most immediately recognisable guitars of its era, and saw action with such notable British bands as the Hollies and the Dave Clark Five.

The most visually appealing Vox body shape was without doubt the rounded lute contours of the "Mk" series. Originally named the Phantom Mk III, it quickly became known as the Vox "Teardrop".

The Teardrop appeared in many different forms – the model shown here is a 12-string electric produced in 1967. The name most commonly associated with these guitars is Brian Jones of the Rolling Stones – indeed, he was rarely pictured playing any other guitar.

It's fair to say that the Teardrop was never the most playable of guitars: with no inward curving on the body, the instrument was difficult to use in a sitting position. However, so strong are its associations with the Swinging Sixties that the Teardrop remains a popular item among retro fetishists. Although some of the rarer originals are now highly collectible, the American-built re-issues are far better as musical instruments.

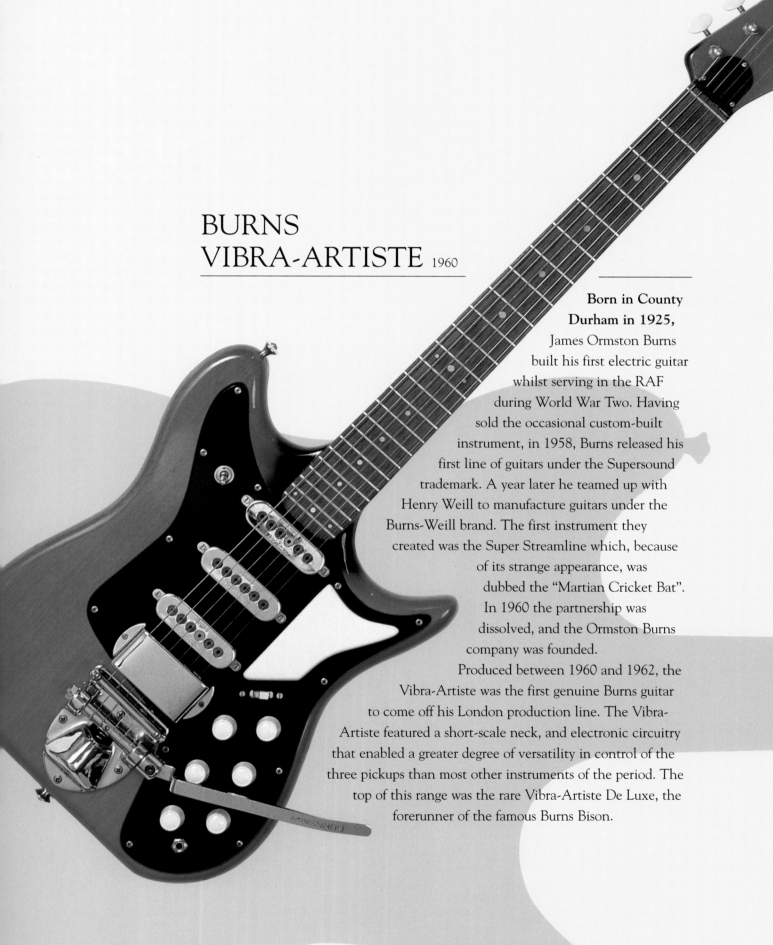

BURNS
VIBRA-ARTISTE 1960

Born in County Durham in 1925, James Ormston Burns built his first electric guitar whilst serving in the RAF during World War Two. Having sold the occasional custom-built instrument, in 1958, Burns released his first line of guitars under the Supersound trademark. A year later he teamed up with Henry Weill to manufacture guitars under the Burns-Weill brand. The first instrument they created was the Super Streamline which, because of its strange appearance, was dubbed the "Martian Cricket Bat". In 1960 the partnership was dissolved, and the Ormston Burns company was founded.

Produced between 1960 and 1962, the Vibra-Artiste was the first genuine Burns guitar to come off his London production line. The Vibra-Artiste featured a short-scale neck, and electronic circuitry that enabled a greater degree of versatility in control of the three pickups than most other instruments of the period. The top of this range was the rare Vibra-Artiste De Luxe, the forerunner of the famous Burns Bison.

BURNS BISON 1961

In 1960, Jim Burns showed a prototype of an instrument with a double cutaway and curved horns to leading British jazz guitarist Ike Isaacs. His reaction was memorable: "It looks like a bloody bison!" Thus was named one of the most famous British guitars ever to go into production.

The first in the range was the four-pickup Black Bison, of which only 49 were ever built. (British guitar folklore has it that the fiftieth ended up as a coffee table.)

1962 saw the introduction of three other Bisons – the Model 2 (shown here), 3 and 4. These differed from the original primarily because they featured a more manageable three pickups.

One interesting feature is the four-way pickup selector, which offered settings for "Bass", "Treble", "Split Sound" and the intriguingly named "Wild Dog".

**The Shadows – and in
particular lead guitarist Hank Marvin –**
were extremely influential in the evolution of British pop,
not only through their music, but for the equipment they were seen
using. Just as their patronage all but launched Vox amplifiers, for many,
Burns guitars will always be strongly associated with the group.
During the late-1950s, the Shadows were – of course – rarely seen parted from their
red Fender Stratocasters: they were among the first prominent champions of the instrument

BURNS MARVIN 1964

outside of the US. However, by 1963 rhythm guitarist Bruce Welch
had began to tire of the persistent intonation and tuning difficulties he was experiencing with
the Strat. Thus, the band began working with Jim Burns on the design of a new instrument. One year and more
than thirty working prototypes later, the resulting Burns Marvin was unveiled.
The Marvin was immediately distinguishable from other Burns guitars by the ornate carved scrolling
of the headstock. Sonically, the fitting of the Rezo-tube system and Rezo-Matic pickups, gave the
guitar an unusually warm sound. Between 1964 and 1965, only 350 of the company's flagship
instrument were built, making it probably the most sought-after British electric guitar ever.
Although Jim Burns was an innovator, he was a much less accomplished
businessman. In September 1965, indebted to their suppliers, Ormston Burns
was bought out by the US music giant, Baldwin. Production of the
Marvin and other designs continued, but it's the pre-takeover
instruments that are of most interest to the vintage
guitar collector.

HOFNER CLUB 60 1958

Germany's most famous manufacturer of stringed instruments was founded in 1897 by Karl Höfner. A violin maker by trade, by 1910 Höfner had already introduced acoustic guitars to his range. By 1930, under the management of his son Walter, Höfner is thought to have been the largest guitar producer in Western Europe. Rock 'n' roll hit Germany earlier than most of Europe, largely thanks to the proliferation of US air bases that had been established after the war, which created a huge demand for electric guitars. Walter Höfner was quick to satisfy the market.

The first range of Hofner (like Hagstrom, the umlaut over the "o" was dropped for the sake of exports) guitars to make a big impression was the Club series. The baby of the team was the cheap-and-cheerful, single-pickup Club 40; the Club 50 was essentially the same instrument with a second pickup added. However, with its attractive flamed body, ebony fingerboard, and extravagant inlays to the headstock and fingerboard, it was the Club 60 that took pride of place in many a music store window.

In appearance, the Club 60 was a straight Les Paul copy, but since it was of hollow construction the guitar was considerably lighter than the original. The body top was arched, and finished with spruce; the back and sides were flame maple. The neck was a five-part construction, using maple, mahogany, beech, and an ebony fingerboard which featured inlays made from mother-of-pearl, fret markers set in rosewood and celluloid strips.

HOFNER 175 ₁₉₆₆

Even though by the mid-1960s, Fenders and Gibsons were increasingly available to European guitarists, the major German manufacturers were still playing it safe, providing variations on well-known designs. In silhouette, the Hofner 175 was barely distinguishable from a Stratocaster. Turn on the lights, however, and you find a delightfully tacky vinyl-covered body with red "pearloid" scratch plate. So great was the demand for cheap electric guitars during this period, that Hofner could – quite literally – not wait for the paint to dry. Covering instruments in a pre-finished vinyl speeded up the process and allowed for what would otherwise be unfeasibly ornate designs.

The 175 featured one master volume and individual tone controls for each of the three pickups. One area in which Hofner guitars were quite unusual was in their preferred use of imbedded "roller pots" rather than conventional knobs. Although these may have been visually neater, they were considerably harder to use.

By the 1970s, Europe had been swamped by cheaper Japanese copies, bringing an end to the European guitar boom.

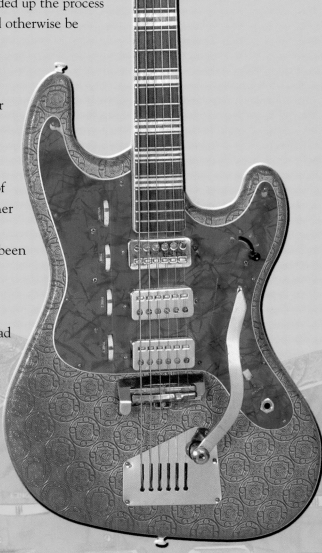

BURNS
SPLIT SONIC 1964

The Sonic range of guitars ran for almost the
full length of the "first" Burns era (1960–65).
The first model in the series was the original
short-scale Sonic. This was followed by the
Split Sonic, a budget version of the relatively
expensive Black Bison. The third member of
the group was the even cheaper Vista Sonic,
which featured "Tri-Sonic" pickups rather
than the "Ultra-Sonic" pickups usually found
on Burns guitars.

BURNS UK FLYTE 1977

Jim Burns was evidently a volatile figure. He would sketch out designs on any scrap of paper that came to hand – even old cigarette packets. Burns employee Les Andrews, remembered: "When we started developing a new guitar, it was from a blank piece of timber, cut roughly in the shape of the body. Jim would then cover it with pencil lines, notes, shading and so on to convey to me what he had in mind…. It took a few days of trial and error before we got a new model, but it worked!"

He was also an irrepressible character. After the failure of his first incarnation, Jim Burns bounced back in 1974 with a new company – Burns UK – and a selection of unusual new designs, among them the rather curious Flyte. Apparently inspired by the Concorde aircraft, the Flyte was a novel variation on the Flying V "arrow" idea. It was not well received and in 1977 the company folded.

Still refusing to be beaten, he made yet another comeback in 1979 with the Jim Burns brand, mixing reissues with more newly designed oddities. Sadly, four years later he was out of business once again.

Although Jim Burns died in 1998, the brand name lives on. In 1992, having won Burns' full consent, young guitar maker Barry Gibson revived the name, producing high-quality versions of Burns originals – even the ill-fated Flyte. After over ten successful years in business, Burns is once again the most significant name in the British guitar world, making a particular impression in 2001 with the award-winning Brian May signature model.

135

TOKAI HUMMING BIRD 1968

Contrary to popular belief, the earliest Japanese electric guitars were not at first mere copies of popular Fender and Gibson models. In fact, the background to Japan's attitude to the electric guitar is in itself quite strange. In one of those peculiar clashes of pop culture, at a time when the Beatles had conquered most of the world, Japanese teenagers were screaming at airports to get a glimpse of a clean-cut US guitar instrumental outfit called The Ventures. (Even now, the Ventures – their surviving original members still going strong – could sell-out Japanese stadiums in the way that Rolling Stones concerts do in the West.)

By the time they arrived in Japan, the Ventures were using US-built Mosrite guitars. Thus, young Japanese guitar wannabees dreaming of owning their own "eleki", were generally not lusting after Teles, Strats, Les Pauls or Gretsches, but the "lopsided" body and angled pickup of the Mosrite – a brand that had not enjoyed great success in its home country.

The Tokai company, based in Hamamatsu, was one of the most important names in the early history of the Japanese guitar. Visually, the Tokai Humming Bird is based strongly on the Mosrite shape, but with the horns styled in a way that gives the guitar a uniquely oriental character.

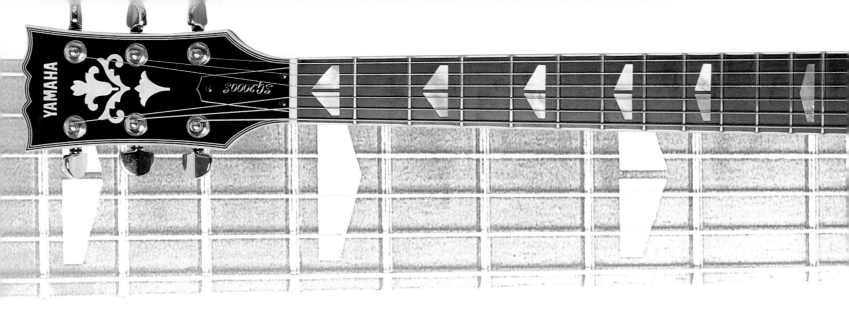

YAMAHA SG2000 1976

From time to time, a single product comes along which completely revolutionises an entire industry. Until 1976, Japanese-built guitars were simply not rated. The prevailing thinking was that these cheap, mass-produced instruments were fine for beginners or impoverished amateurs, but you'd never see a professional playing one. It's no exaggeration to say that the Yamaha SG2000 turned

this notion upside down. For the first time it was shown that in terms of quality a Japanese-built production model could not only compete, but could wipe the floor with the traditional US competition.

Yamaha was founded in 1887, and began making acoustic guitars after the end of the war. The first Yamaha production electric guitar emerged in 1966. Like other

Japanese makers of the time, it looked to Mosrite for inspiration. During the following years, Yamaha gained a reputation for producing slightly eccentric – if reasonable quality – takes on the Gibson Les Paul shape.

Perhaps the most surprising aspect of the SG2000's design is that it looks so "normal", eschewing the needless gimmickry often previously found on

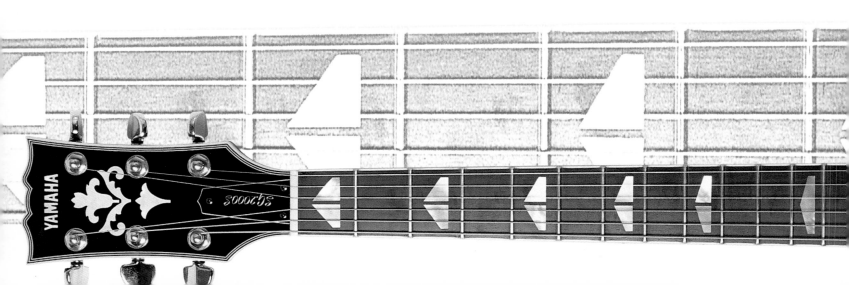

Japanese guitars. What we have here is essentially a Les Paul Standard, with a double cutaway – not a million miles removed from Gibson double-necks of the late 1950s – but carefully redesigned and assembled using state-of-the-art construction techniques of the day: a fine blend of old and new.

Like the Les Paul, the SG2000 featured carved maple on a mahogany body. But unlike the flat back of the original, the Yamaha was contoured in a way that made it extremely comfortable to wear. A brass block was set into the maple beneath the bridge to improve sustain. Particularly unusual for a six-string guitar, the SG2000 featured a multi-laminate "through" neck built from a central strip of maple surrounded by mahogany.

Popular wisdom of the period was that genuine Gibson guitars were no longer being built to the exacting standards of yore. When former Gibson endorsee Carlos Santana made the SG2000 his main instrument, the battle was won. The SG2000 has remained in production ever since, making it that rarest of creatures, a genuine "modern classic".

SHERGOLD MASQUERADER 1979

Shergold was the last British-made brand to be produced in any great quantity. Established in the mid-1960 by ex-Burns employees Jack Golder and Norman Holder, the company spent the next decade producing guitars and spare parts for other trade names. Frustrated by this way of working, in 1976, Golder and Holder set out to establish Shergold as a quality name in its own right. Although the guitars may have been mass-produced, Shergold presented itself as craftsmanlike cottage industry – a view reflected in its logo shield of the chisel-wielding artisan.

Shergold guitars were modelled on the Hayman range the company had previously produced as a "trade" brand. The instruments had a quality feel and sound, but despite such exotic finishes as the distinctive apple green sunburst, they were not considered the most stylish kids on the block. However, what *could* be said was that they were not mere copies of the American classics. This singularity extended to the use of an unusual African hardwood called *obechi* in a number of their bodies.

Shergold's two most successful six-string guitar were the Masquerader (seen here) and the Modulator. Like all Shergolds, both came equipped with a tacky black plastic bridge cover, which most players found rather ugly and removed (and subsequently lost). The Modulator was especially daring in that it was designed to work with a series of slot-in electronic modules kitted out with different combinations of switches and tone controls – some even allowing for different sound effects or for the output of stereo (or even quadraphonic) signals.

The Shergold production finally line ran out of steam in 1981. After a decade of little activity, the brand was resuscitated briefly in 1991, but folded a year following the death of Jack Golder.

TOKAI TST-5O 1985

This range of Tokai Stratocaster copies is thought to have been responsible for Fender's decision to consider producing low-cost models outside of the US. Tokai began producing "Strats" in 1976. Although vastly cheaper than Fender production models, the Tokais were not "knock-offs" like other Japanese copies of the time, but had originally been intended to make classic-style Strats available to Japanese buyers at an affordable price. However, demand quickly followed in the West.

Early Tokai Strats were as good as the "real thing". Indeed, they had all the features of an original Strat with the bonus of a five-way selector switch – Fender players of the past had devised numerous ways of "jamming" the three-way switch so that combinations of the back and middle, and front and middle pickups could be heard.

To add insult to injury, the Japanese manufacturer cheekily aped the Fender logo on the headstock, a feature that was later dropped following legal action. (Where the word "Stratocaster" would have appeared alongside the logo, on the Tokai is printed "Springy Sound", in an identical typeface.)

8

MODERN SOLIDS

THE 1970S SAW THE BIG GUNS IN DECLINE. FENDERS AND GIBSONS HAD LOST THEIR QUALITY EDGE AND OLD ATTITUDES WERE BEING UPTURNED, AS JAPANESE GUITARS WENT FROM STRENGTH TO STRENGTH. THE STRATOCASTER MAY STILL HAVE BEEN KING, BUT A NEW GENERATION OF ROCK PLAYERS BEGAN TO LOOK FOR IMPROVEMENTS ON THE ORIGINAL DESIGN. THUS THE "SUPERSTRAT" WAS BORN.

JACKSON SOLOIST 1981

Californian Grover Jackson is widely credited with
inventing the concept of the so-called Superstrat.
However, he owes some of this success to a man named
Wayne Charvel, who during the mid-1970s established a
bold new venture, providing spare parts that would
enable players to soup-up their production-line guitars.
In 1978, with business not quite booming, Charvel sold
out to guitar maker Jackson. The company took off in
1980 when Randy Rhoads – Ozzy Osbourne's brilliant
young guitarist – approached Jackson to build him a
custom guitar. This evolved into the Soloist, the first
production Superstrat.

The body of the Soloist is clearly derived from the
classic Stratocaster shape, albeit with extended horns
on the upper bout. However, rather than using a bolt-
on neck *a la* Fender, the neck and body centre are
machined from a single piece of maple; the "wings"
are made from softer poplar. This rather more costly
approach to construction was used for a while at
Gibson on mid-1960s guitars such as the Firebird. The
Soloist, like pretty well all Superstrats that have
followed, pioneered the idea of a two-octave
fingerboard – three more frets than are found on a
standard Stratocaster.

Although the Soloist is clearly derivative in design,
Jackson came up with what has effectively become his own
visual trademark – the angular, pointed headstock. Yet even
that has a clear antecedent in the ill-fated Gibson Explorer,
produced briefly in 1958.

Jackson made the Soloist available in a wide variety of
pickup combinations, and in 1990 added a range of exotic
finishes, among them the "California Sunset" shown here.

PAUL REED SMITH
STANDARD 24 ₁₉₈₅

It was while at university in 1975 that Paul Reed Smith fulfilled a childhood ambition of making an electric guitar. Giving up his mathematics degree course, Reed began producing his own custom models – unfortunately, he found selling them a good deal more difficult. During a period working at Danny Gatton's repair shop in New York, Reed Smith made an important realisation: "All the top guitarists were playing either Gibsons or Fenders… I decided that if I was going to be successful, I needed to combine the best features of both." In 1983, Smith came up with what he saw as the perfect compromise, a body shape, construction and sound that would appeal both to Stratocaster and Les Paul players alike.

Having in some way interested such diverse parties as Ovation, Guild, Kramer and Yamaha, Reed Smith finally decided to set up his own production line in his home town of Annapolis, Maryland: the following year, the PRS Custom made its first appearance. It provided a visual template for the vast majority of PRS guitars that have followed.

Among the early users was Carlos Santana – who remains the most famous PRS champion.

CHARVEL SPECTRUM 1989

The Charvel brand is sometimes seen as a footnote to the more significant story of Jackson guitars. In fact, the first Charvels appeared in 1979, predating the Jackson debut by two years. However, by the time this 1989 Spectrum appeared, Wayne Charvel had long departed the company, and the instruments bearing his name were a Japanese-built diffusion range for the US-built Jackson Superstrats. Evidently somewhat miffed at the degree to which Grover Jackson took the plaudits during the 1980s, Charvel has enjoyed some recent success with this own range of instruments – under the Wayne brand.

The principal difference between the early Jacksons and Charvels lay in the neck construction. Being of the bolt-on variety, Charvels were more affordable than their "sister" brand: indeed, it could be argued that Charvels were critical to the whole Superstrat phenomenon. The Spectrum is interesting in that it offers a slightly unusual fusion of modern and vintage characteristics. For a start, it has a 22-fret fingerboard (unlike the more common two octaves found on Jacksons). Furthermore, the pickguard is quite clearly inspired by those found on the original Fender Precision bass guitars. And there's the headstock – angled in quite the opposite direction to the characteristic Jackson "drooper". The three pickups are connected using Jackson's JE-1500 active circuitry – although the pickups themselves are not active.

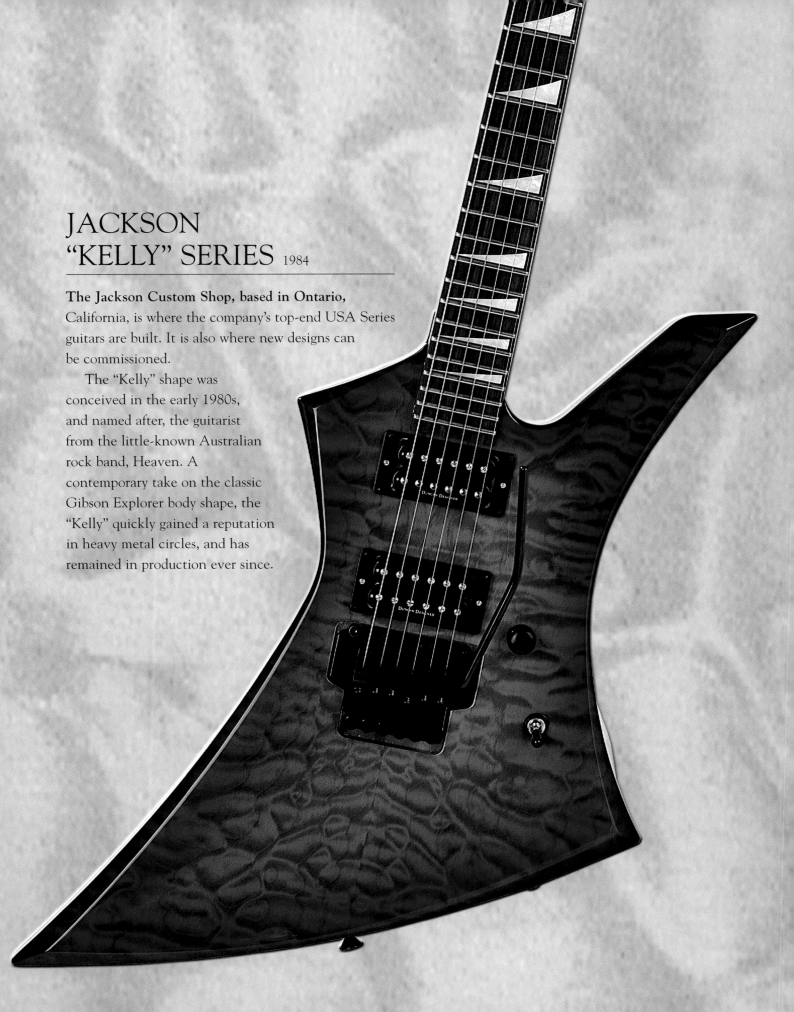

JACKSON
"KELLY" SERIES 1984

The Jackson Custom Shop, based in Ontario, California, is where the company's top-end USA Series guitars are built. It is also where new designs can be commissioned.

The "Kelly" shape was conceived in the early 1980s, and named after, the guitarist from the little-known Australian rock band, Heaven. A contemporary take on the classic Gibson Explorer body shape, the "Kelly" quickly gained a reputation in heavy metal circles, and has remained in production ever since.

JACKSON WARRIOR PRO 1990

During the latter half of the 1980s, Jackson began to evolve from the Superstrat market in which their reputation had first been forged. The Warrior is one of the most exotic designs to come out of the Jackson Custom shop. A highly-specified instrument, the Warrior featured a "build-through" neck, ebony fingerboard with characteristic Jackson "shark fin" inlays, "jumbo" frets, Seymour Duncan humbucking pickups and a Floyd Rose locking tremolo system. This model is shown with the unusual diagonal fingerboard cut, with the pickups similarly angled – production models feature the more regular perpendicular cut.

Almost insect-like in dramatic black, the various Warrior models can be ordered from a list of over fifty lavish custom finishes.

At the end of 2002, the Jackson and Charvel brands came under the ownership of the mighty Fender corporation. Only time will tell how this will impact on what is arguably the most significant name in rock guitar of the past two decades.

IBANEZ
ICEMAN IC210 1979

The Ibanez story began in 1908, when the Hoshino music store first opened in Nagoya, Japan. In 1954, Hoshino began distributing Spanish acoustic guitars under the Ibanez brand. Eight years later, the company purchased the rights to the Ibanez name, and quickly began to carve out a reputation manufacturing some of the most impressive Fender and Gibson "copies". This era came to an abrupt end in 1976 when Gibson's parent company took legal action claiming a trademark infringement relating to their use of the patented Les Paul headstock. Although the matter was eventually settled out of court, thereafter Ibanez set about taking a more innovatory tack. (Ironically, some of the so-called Ibanez "Lawsuit" instruments made during this period are worth more to collectors than the "originals".)

The Iceman was one of the first "new" Ibanez models. Unusual in appearance, its body styling combines echoes of the Gibson Reverse Firebird with the accentuated lower horn of a Rickenbacker bass. An unusual features of the control panel is the four-way rotary tone selector knob.

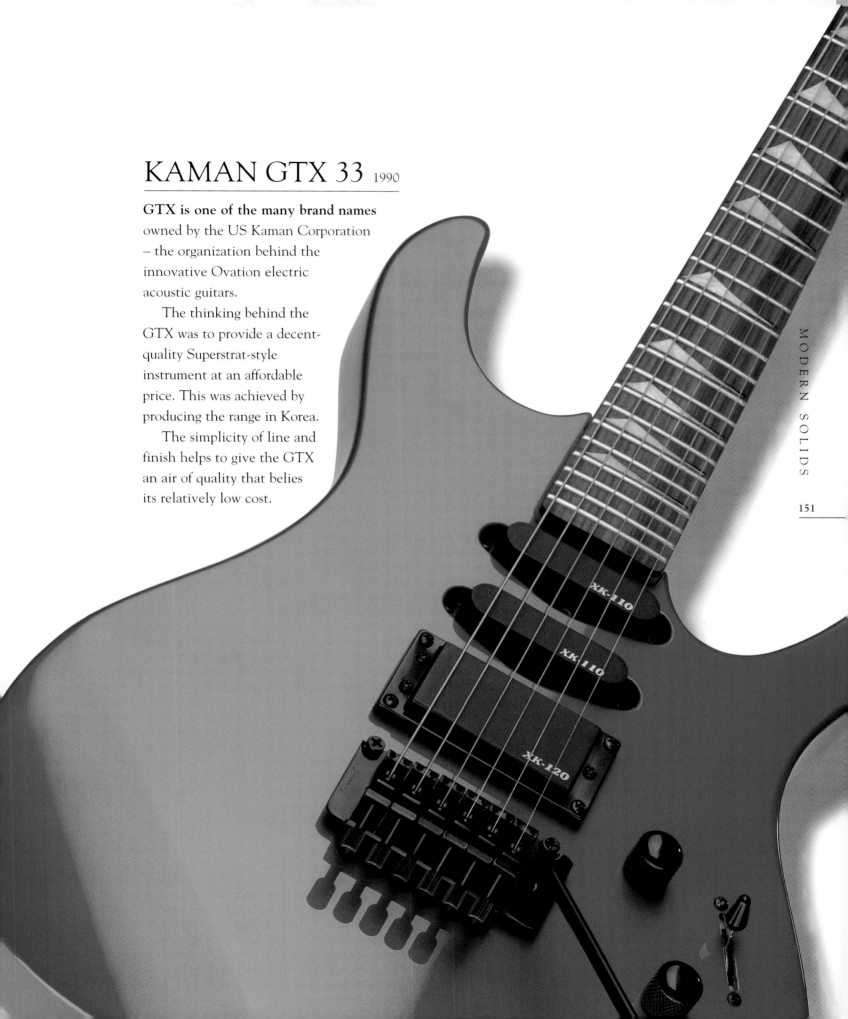

KAMAN GTX 33 1990

GTX is one of the many brand names owned by the US Kaman Corporation – the organization behind the innovative Ovation electric acoustic guitars.

The thinking behind the GTX was to provide a decent-quality Superstrat-style instrument at an affordable price. This was achieved by producing the range in Korea.

The simplicity of line and finish helps to give the GTX an air of quality that belies its relatively low cost.

PAUL REED SMITH DRAGON 2000 1999

With its richly ornate body, the Paul Reed Smith Dragon series is without doubt a design classic. It's also the most collectible of modern guitars: the series are made in extremely small numbers (between fifty and a hundred of each one) and retail at a hefty price – you're unlikely to see too much change from $20,000. The first Dragon appeared in 1992. Periodically, new models – with differing dragon motifs – are introduced. The model shown here is a prototype for the Dragon 2000.

The PRS Dragon is part of an ongoing dream fulfilment for Smith, who recalls: "I knew I wanted to make guitars when I was 16. I even had a poster on my wall that said 'Les Paul Custom Dragon.' Someday, I was going to build Dragon guitars."

Of course, the idea of decorating musical instruments is not a new one – tacky airbrushed images have been adorning guitars since the 1960s. But good taste aside, the difference here is that the Dragon's appearance is created using inlays of such amazing intricacy that each guitar really is a work of art. Indeed, the PRS Dragon has been given the ultimate recognition of a place in the Smithsonian Institute.

IBANEZ JEM 1987

Despite having produced some distinctive, high-quality models, by the mid-1980s the Ibanez name was still associated with derivative guitars. In an attempt to alter this perception, parent company Hoshino set up a US wing, aimed at recruiting star talent. The first player targeted was Steve Vai. Their approach was simple: they researched Vai's tastes in guitars, produced a one-off of what they thought would be his perfect guitar, wrapped it up and sent it to him as a Christmas present! Vai's response was so positive that he spent the next three months refining the design. The result was the 1987 Jem, a high-performance Superstrat with a locking tremolo, three custom-designed DiMarzio pickups, and a two-octave scalloped fingerboard. A magnificent versatile instrument, the Jem is arguably one of the finest production-line guitars ever made.

One unusual aspect of the Jem's design is the "monkeygrip" carrying handle. However, what made the Jem so distinctive was the variety of outlandish finishes along with intricate matching fretboard inlays.

IBANEZ UNIVERSE 1989

Coinciding with Steve Vai's elevation to the status of rock guitar icon, the Jem was a massive success, helping Ibanez carve out a reputation as a manufacturer of distinctive instruments. To the present day, there have been over a dozen different models produced.

One interesting – although less successful – development was the Ibanez Universe. Vai wanted a guitar with an increased bass range. The result was the seven-string Universe, a modified Jem with an additional bass string tuned to the note "B" below "Bottom E". The idea of adding a seventh string was not actually that new. Jazz guitarist George Van Eps had pioneered this approach with his own Epiphone "Epi Deluxe" in the 1940s. Although this failed to catch on, he reworked the idea again in the 1960s, this time with a Gretsch guitar.

Like those two curiosities, the Universe was not a commercial winner: it seems that for most guitarists, mastering six strings was already more than enough of a challenge.

PARKER FLY 1993

One of the most significant guitars of the late twentieth century, the Parker Fly proves that it's possible to come up with a radical contemporary take on the design and construction of the solid-body electric guitar. Designed in 1991 by Ken Parker and Larry Fishman, as futuristic as the Fly may appear visually, at its core are ideas that return to the guitar's early origins. Ken Parker explains: "I think of this guitar as harking back to things like Renaissance lutes, which would have soft woods veneered in ebony. "We're doing the same thing, with modern materials."

From the earliest solid-body experimenters in the 1940s to Ned Steinberger's revolutionary "graphite" guitars, the conventional wisdom was to construct instruments whose bodies were as dense and free from natural resonance as possible: hence,

hardwoods such as alder, ash and mahogany have always been most commonly used. Parker turns this idea on its head by building the core of the body from a highly resonant softwood – poplar. This is then covered in a rigid plastic outer skin that not only provides extreme strength, but also allows the instrument to resonate to a far greater degree than other solid-body guitars – a fact that is evident when the guitar is played "unplugged". A similar neck construction makes the Fly a fabulously light weight guitar.

As well as featuring two humbucking pickups, the Fly also has Piezo pickups built into the bridge. This takes full advantage of the guitar's resonance, producing a natural acoustic sound.

PATRICK EGGLE BERLIN SERIES 1992

A graduate of the Musical
Instrument Technology course at
the London College of Furniture,
Patrick Eggle started building guitars
professionally in 1983. In 1991 he set up his
first small machine shop in a Hertfordshire barn
and started building the Patrick Eggle Climaxe.
With financial backing, a year later he was able to
move into factory premises, and the Climaxe guitar
was renamed the Berlin. Eggle quickly earned a
reputation as one of Europe's leading guitar makers, his
instruments being particularly rated for the versatility of
their sound – indeed, Eggle has been called
the English Paul Reed Smith.

At the end of the 1990s, frustrated by
the demands of managing a growing
business which gave him less and less
time to design and build guitars, Eggle
resigned from his own company. He now
concentrates on producing custom
instruments under the Patrick James
Eggle brand.

ERNIE BALL MUSICMAN EVH 1992

In 1965, Leo Fender sold his pioneering business to the CBS Corporation. Five years later he joined forces with former employees who had formed MusicMan. In spite of such a weighty heritage, MusicMan didn't quite enjoy the level of success some might have expected, and in 1984 the company was acquired by Ernie Ball, one of the biggest names in guitar strings.

In the late 1980s, Ernie Ball MusicMan got together with Eddie Van Halen, the decade's greatest guitar hero, to produce a new signature model. Like many of the "super-guitars" before and since, what Van Halen had in mind was a cross between a Strat and a Les Paul. The resulting EVH signature model was an attractively simple, high-spec instrument based broadly around the company's 1987 Silhouette model. The body was carved from basswood and featured an exotic "quilted" maple top. The EVH was available in a variety of finishes, the one shown here is the Trans-Gold Quilt. The electrics featured a pair of custom zebra-striped DiMarzio humbuckers and a single "tone" control.

In the mid-90s, Van Halen defected to Peavey and, although barely ten years old, the original signature model is already a hot collectors item.

9
SPECIALS

JUDGING BY THE ENDURING POPULARITY OF MODELS DESIGNED OVER FIFTY YEARS AGO, IT COULD BE ARGUED THAT GUITARISTS ARE A CONSERVATIVE BUNCH. YET THERE HAVE ALWAYS BEEN CRAFTSMEN WHO HAVE SOUGHT TO PRODUCE UNIQUE, ONE-OF-A-KIND INSTRUMENTS; WHILST OTHERS HAVE LOOKED TO TECHNOLOGY FOR WAYS TO PROPEL THE GUITAR INTO THE NEXT CENTURY.

KRUNDAAL
BIKINI 1960

Designed in 1960 by Wandre Pioli
of the Italian Davoli company, this
mini modernist masterpiece lays
claim to being the first ever self-
contained electric guitar.

Like many other early Italian
electric guitars, the Krundaal Bikini
exhibits a body styling unlike
anything that was being produced
elsewhere in the world at that time.
The most notable feature of this
instrument is the "egg" that fits
snugly into the body's lower
bout: this is, in fact, a
built-in amplifier and
8-inch speaker. The
battery power pack is
concealed in the hollow
body of the guitar.

GODWIN
GUITAR ORGAN 1976

The 1960s saw the birth of the first electronic effects, such as fuzz boxes and wah-wah pedals. As these proliferated some manufacturers came up with the bright idea of integrating these sounds into their guitars. In 1966, the British Vox company produced the first so-called "guitar-organ", which integrated the circuitry of the popular Vox Continental organ into a Vox Phantom guitar. The most successful attempt was made a decade or so later by Godwin in Italy. The operating principle was simple: each fret was wired up to a tone generator; when the string touched against that fret it completed an electronic circuit which produced a note. The body of the Godwin was almost as deep as that of an acoustic guitar: this was necessary to house the circuit boards. Consequently, the instrument was rather heavy. The control panel features a mammoth 19 switches and 13 knobs.

As impressive as this instrument could sound, the concept of a guitar/organ was largely viewed as a novelty, and few were used to any great extent.

FRAMUS SUPERYOB 1974

Formed in Wolverhampton at the end of the 1960s, Slade were a powerful, hard-rocking band with
an aggressive "skinhead" image. But although they quickly acquired a formidable live reputation, they
could barely give their records away. By 1972, the suede heads and Doc Martens boots had been replaced
by long hair, bushy sideburns and glitter galore. Slade became Britain's biggest chart band of the era. In
particular, guitarist Dave Hill is fondly remembered for his increasingly outlandish attire on TV's *Top of
the Pops*. It was in 1973 that British guitar maker John Birch was commissioned to create a custom
instrument that would be appropriate for Hill's new stage persona. The result was the Super Yob, a
cartoon Smith and Wesson straight out of the Wild West, that evokes perfectly the "post-psychedelic"
design of the era. A year later, a similar guitar was produced by German company Framus.

REBETH CROSS 1982

British luthier Barry Collier clearly had the occult-obsessive metal guitarist in mind when he designed this instrument. The ornate woodwork and the brass fittings found on the body have been given a deliberately crude finish that creates an almost Gothic effect.

Little is known about Collier's Rebeth brand name other than he used it on a very limited number of custom guitars produced during the early 1980s.

BRIAN MAY "RED SPECIAL" 1964

Abandoning a PhD in astronomy to go full-time with Queen, Brian May could never be described as a run-of-the-mill rock star. Whilst guitarists happily while away the hours arguing the merits of "Strats versus Les Pauls", the issue has always been less relevant to May: the guitar he used on every Queen album and tour is one he designed and built himself as a teenager.

May and his father began work on the "Red Special" in 1962. A carefully considered project from the outset, the guitarist recalls: "We tried to design a solid-body guitar that had all the advantages of a hollowbody – the ability to feed back in just the right way."

The oak body was carved from a five hundred year-old fireplace mantel. The neck was much wider than usual, to accommodate May's large fingers. The electronics were also odd in that each pickup had its own on/off and phase switches, providing a wider spectrum of tones than other guitars.

In 2001, the London-based Burns company launched a signature version of the Red Special to considerable critical acclaim. It quickly established itself as one of the most popular solid-body guitars on the market.

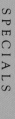

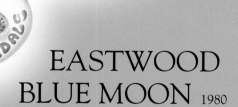

EASTWOOD
BLUE MOON 1980

Lancastrian guitar builder and repairer Brian Eastwood created this truly
unusual instrument in 1980 for the UK rock 'n' roll band Showaddywaddy. It was used
widely in the promotion of their hit single "Blue Moon".

Although it was firmly intended as a novelty instrument, it is in fact a perfectly playable guitar.
Among its more interesting features, the machine heads are built into the body of the guitar, the
strings being anchored in position behind the huge silver star on the headstock. No pickup is
visible on the top of the body; to maintain the visual effect it is concealed beneath the surface.

Eastwood has also created an acoustic version of the Blue Moon design.

ROB ARMSTRONG "CORNFLAKE" 1979

Firmly established for decades as one of Britain's leading acoustic guitar makers, Rob Armstrong can number such noted pickers as George Harrison, Bert Jansch and Gordon Giltrap among his clients.

Armstrong, himself, admits: "I've always liked messing about with the unconventional side of guitar making." His instruments, however, are especially prized for their innovatory approach to acoustics rather than any novelty value.

One exception, perhaps, is this "Cornflake" model, commissioned in 1979 by Simon Nicol of British folk-rockers Fairport Convention. Armstrong took apart a cheap Columbus Les Paul copy and replaced the body with a solid block of wood cut to the same size as a serial packet. A particularly nice touch is the amusing brand logo on the headstock.

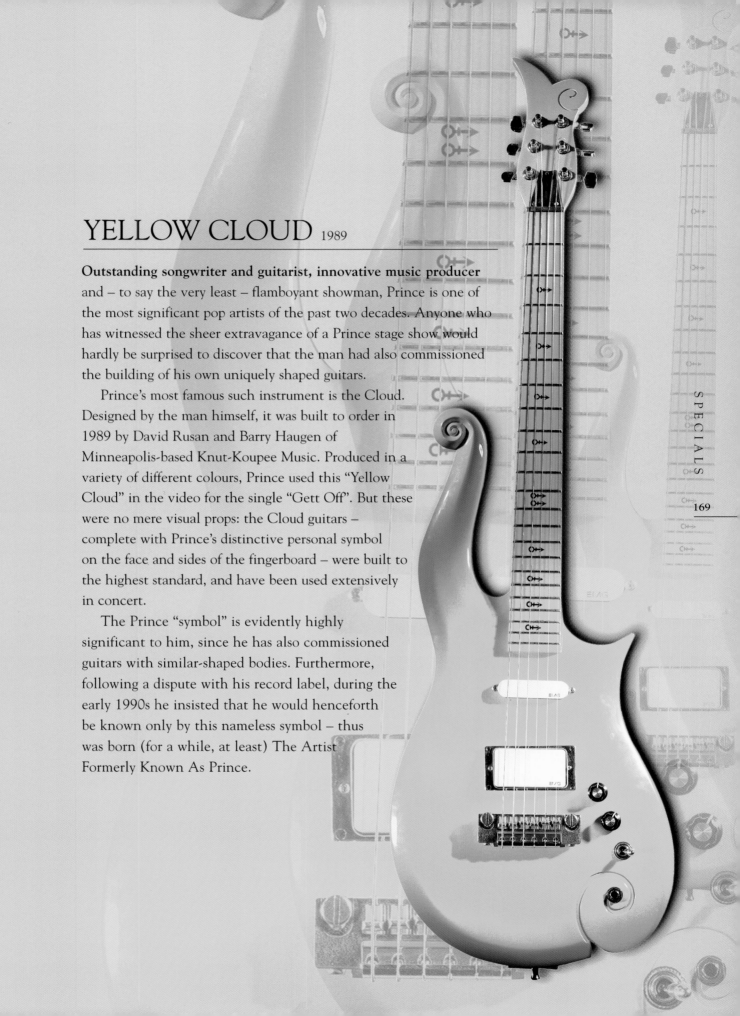

YELLOW CLOUD 1989

Outstanding songwriter and guitarist, innovative music producer
and – to say the very least – flamboyant showman, Prince is one of
the most significant pop artists of the past two decades. Anyone who
has witnessed the sheer extravagance of a Prince stage show would
hardly be surprised to discover that the man had also commissioned
the building of his own uniquely shaped guitars.

Prince's most famous such instrument is the Cloud.
Designed by the man himself, it was built to order in
1989 by David Rusan and Barry Haugen of
Minneapolis-based Knut-Koupee Music. Produced in a
variety of different colours, Prince used this "Yellow
Cloud" in the video for the single "Gett Off". But these
were no mere visual props: the Cloud guitars –
complete with Prince's distinctive personal symbol
on the face and sides of the fingerboard – were built to
the highest standard, and have been used extensively
in concert.

The Prince "symbol" is evidently highly
significant to him, since he has also commissioned
guitars with similar-shaped bodies. Furthermore,
following a dispute with his record label, during the
early 1990s he insisted that he would henceforth
be known only by this nameless symbol – thus
was born (for a while, at least) The Artist
Formerly Known As Prince.

YAMAHA G10 1988

The 1980s was the decade that saw the emerging dominance of the synthesiser and digital technology. Yet even before the electronic dance music revolution, a significant proportion of mainstream hit records were being produced using drum machines and synthesisers. For a while, at least, it seemed as if the guitar had fallen from grace. This upsurge in the use of technology was fuelled by the universal adoption of the Musical Instrument Digital Interface (MIDI), a "language" that allowed synthesisers, drum machines and sequencers to communicate with each other.

Yamaha had already produced the world-beating DX7 polysynthesiser; the G10 was an attempt to allow guitarists the luxury of playing such sounds from a guitar-like instrument. In effect a "mute" controller, the G10 made no sound of its own, but could be used to "trigger" notes on any MIDI-compatible synth.

The G10 was a complex instrument that offered highly expressive possibilities – far greater than could be achieved on a regular keyboard – to those prepared to make the effort. Few, however, did, and the G10 was dropped within a year.

SYNTHAXE 1984

A more radical approach to MIDI control came from the British-built SynthAxe. On this instrument, the strings themselves act as the sensors, with microprocessors able to accurately determine notes (and pitch bends) by passing a current through each string and measuring electromagnetic changes using "hard-wired" frets. One immediate peculiarity is that the frets are all equally spaced and the strings are the same gauge. Unlike regular guitars, string tension has no bearing on the pitch of the note transmitted, meaning the SynthAxe doesn't require tuning.

An impressive, if complex, piece of gear, the SynthAxe found fans in jazz-rock players Al Di Meola and Allan Holdsworth, but retailing at close to £10,000 it was always going to have limited appeal.

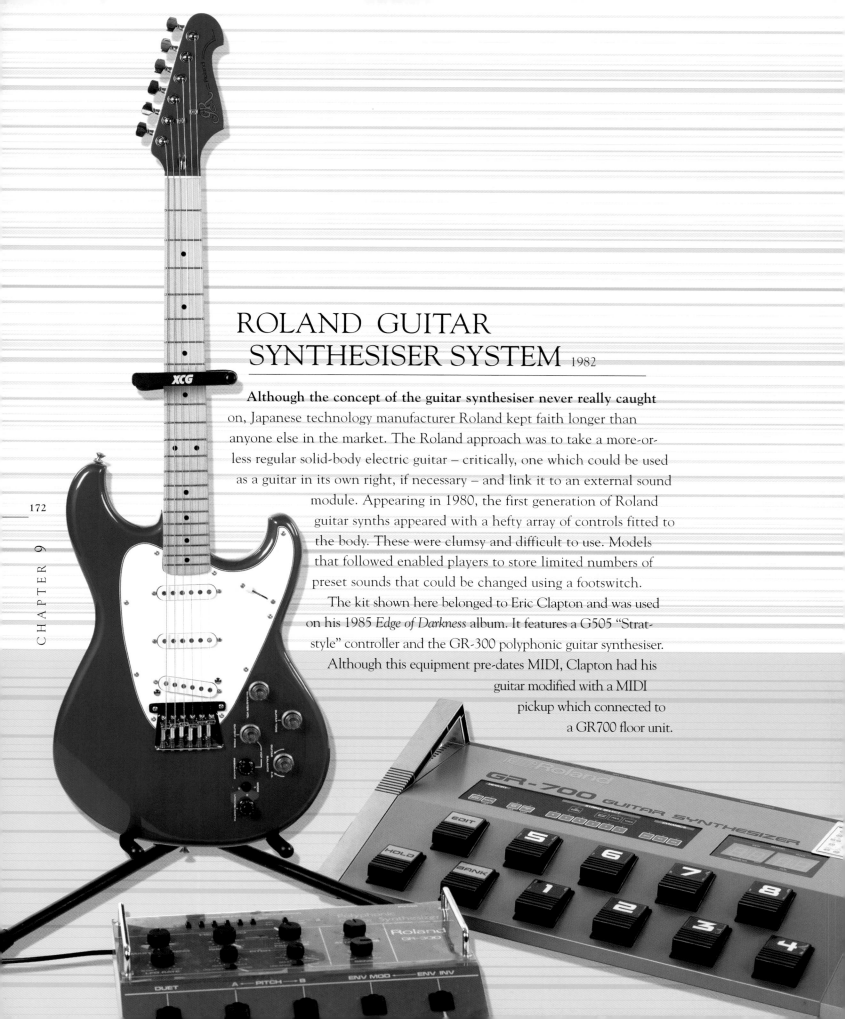

ROLAND GUITAR
SYNTHESISER SYSTEM 1982

Although the concept of the guitar synthesiser never really caught on, Japanese technology manufacturer Roland kept faith longer than anyone else in the market. The Roland approach was to take a more-or-less regular solid-body electric guitar – critically, one which could be used as a guitar in its own right, if necessary – and link it to an external sound module. Appearing in 1980, the first generation of Roland guitar synths appeared with a hefty array of controls fitted to the body. These were clumsy and difficult to use. Models that followed enabled players to store limited numbers of preset sounds that could be changed using a footswitch.

The kit shown here belonged to Eric Clapton and was used on his 1985 *Edge of Darkness* album. It features a G505 "Strat-style" controller and the GR-300 polyphonic guitar synthesiser. Although this equipment pre-dates MIDI, Clapton had his guitar modified with a MIDI pickup which connected to a GR700 floor unit.

ROLAND G707 1984

When MIDI became the global connection standard for musical instruments, the potential was opened up for any suitably kitted guitar to control any MIDI-equipped unit. This meant that MIDI guitars could be used to play synthesisers, drum machines, digital samplers, or program MIDI sequencers. Roland guitars took a different approach to their competitors, in that their internal circuitry took the pitch of the string and converted it into a MIDI value. Although this was a simpler idea, it was also less reliable and the conversion process sometimes resulted in a perceptible delay.

The G707 was the last of Roland's specially made MIDI guitars. The distinctive metal stabilising rod linking the headstock to the body was intended to keep the neck rigid, so that cleaner pitch signals would be transferred to the external control unit. However this also created a rather odd visual effect that potential buyers evidently found off-putting.

Thereafter, Roland stopped making purpose-built MIDI guitars, in favour of systems that used MIDI pickups that could be fitted to any regular electric guitar.

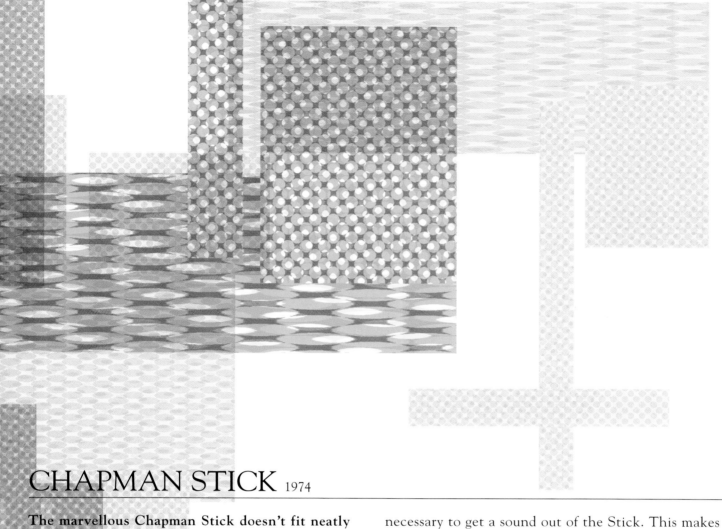

CHAPMAN STICK 1974

The marvellous Chapman Stick doesn't fit neatly into any single category. Some might argue that it isn't even a guitar, since playing technique owe more to the piano than any stringed instrument.

Invented in the late 1960s by Emmett Chapman, and first produced commercially five years later, the Stick is a 10-string electric fretted instrument. Where it differs from a guitar or bass is that the strings are tapped between the frets instead of being plucked, picked or strummed. Where it takes two hands to make a sound on a regular guitar – one to fret the string; one to strike it – only one hand is

necessary to get a sound out of the Stick. This makes it possible to play simultaneous separate lines or chords with each hand. The fingerboard is effectively separated into two halves, with a "bass" side and a "melody" side each played by a different hand. The Stick has a total range of over five octaves – far greater than any guitar.

A cult instrument, the Stick's reputation has been able to grow steadily over the past thirty years, largely through Emmett Chapman's own persistence, and is now well established on the fringes of the guitar fraternity.

10

BASS GUITARS

UNTIL 1951, AND THE LAUNCH OF THE FENDER PRECISION, THE GUITAR AND DOUBLE BASS HAD NO SHARED HERITAGE. THE DOUBLE BASS, THE INSTRUMENT MOST USED FOR LOW-REGISTER PLAYING EVOLVED FROM THE *VIOL DE GAMBA*, A LARGE, STRINGED INSTRUMENT. HOWEVER, BY THE END OF THE DECADE, THE BASS GUITAR HAD ALMOST UNIVERSALLY REPLACED IT.

FENDER PRECISION 1951

Had Leo Fender only invented the Broadcaster (Telecaster) and Stratocaster guitars, his name would still be among the most hallowed in the history of the modern guitar. Yet we often overlook what may well have been his most enduring contribution to the music of the half-century that followed: Leo Fender also invented the bass guitar.

In 1951, he applied the same principles that had successfully introduced the first mass-produced solid-body electric guitar to the double bass. The result was the Fender Precision. Like the Broadcaster, it was essentially a slab of ash with a maple neck – it was just a bit bigger, longer, and had fatter strings.

Given the Precision's chronological position in the early Fender hierarchy, the body shape really does appear to be somewhere between the Telecaster and Stratocaster guitars. The lower bout and upper bout beneath the neck are in very similar proportions to the Tele; the "horn" above the fingerboard provides a glimpse of the possible next stage in Fender body styling.

The Precision enjoyed many advantages over an acoustic double bass, not least that it was more capable of competing with other amplified instruments and more convenient to transport. Of course, from a musician's point of view it was also somewhat easier to play: with a fretted fingerboard, playing in tune – a skill that could take the fret-free double bassist considerable time to perfect – was simplicity itself.

The Precision was such a radical invention that by the end of the 1950s the vast majority of modern music – jazz excepted – had switched from double bass to bass guitar.

One question we might ponder is the extent to which Fender's invention has influenced the way in which music has been produced over the last half-century. All but a tiny proportion of pop and rock has been underpinned by the sound of a bass guitar. Can we imagine the riffing of heavy rock, the depth of reggae or the thrash of punk having anything like the same degree of power had double basses been used?

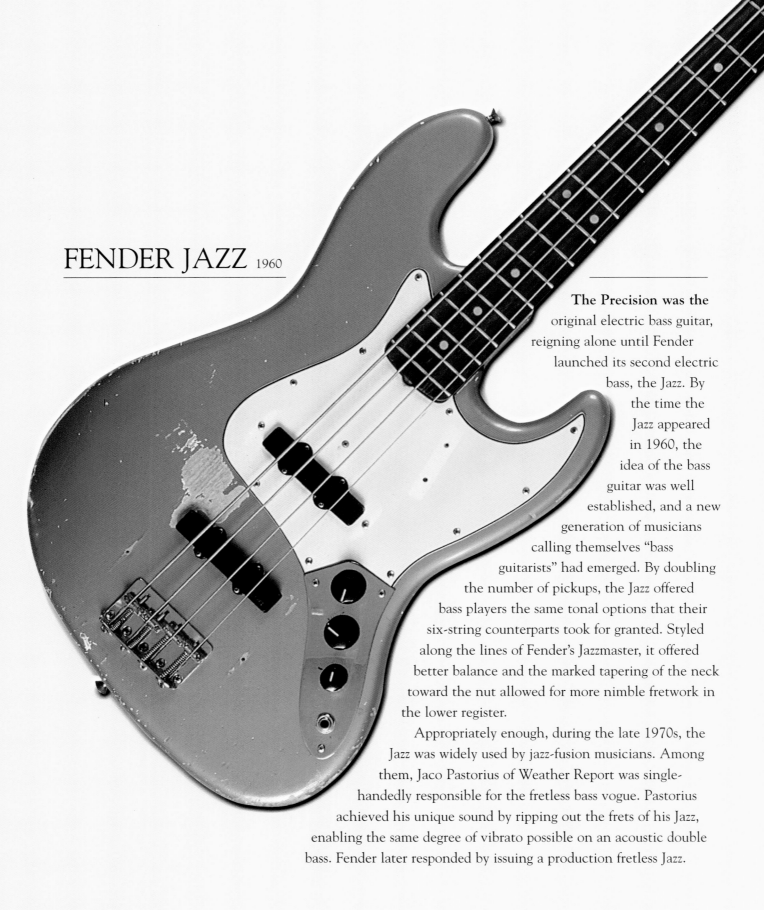

FENDER JAZZ 1960

The Precision was the original electric bass guitar, reigning alone until Fender launched its second electric bass, the Jazz. By the time the Jazz appeared in 1960, the idea of the bass guitar was well established, and a new generation of musicians calling themselves "bass guitarists" had emerged. By doubling the number of pickups, the Jazz offered bass players the same tonal options that their six-string counterparts took for granted. Styled along the lines of Fender's Jazzmaster, it offered better balance and the marked tapering of the neck toward the nut allowed for more nimble fretwork in the lower register.

Appropriately enough, during the late 1970s, the Jazz was widely used by jazz-fusion musicians. Among them, Jaco Pastorius of Weather Report was single-handedly responsible for the fretless bass vogue. Pastorius achieved his unique sound by ripping out the frets of his Jazz, enabling the same degree of vibrato possible on an acoustic double bass. Fender later responded by issuing a production fretless Jazz.

RICKENBACKER 4001 1961

Rickenbacker launched its first bass guitar, the 4000
model, in 1957. Unsurprisingly, given the distinctiveness
of their 6-string electrics, the 4000 was also something
of an oddity. For starters, the body shape was unlike any
other bass guitar on the market, the long horn on the
upper bout protruding almost as far as the 12th fret.
Similarly, construction was different from the
increasingly popular Fender Precision; instead of using
a bolt-on neck, a central block, from headstock to lower
bout, was cut from a single piece of mahogany; the top
and the bottom "wings" of the body were glued on
separately. In 1961, the now-classic twin-pickup 4001
model was introduced.

Unusually, the 4001 has more of a cult
following in the UK than in its
homeland, and was favoured by such
eminent British players as Paul
McCartney and Chris Squire.
The model shown here is from
the early 1970s.

HOFNER 500/1 "VIOLIN BASS" 1957

Young and impoverished
British musicians of the late-1950s rarely had the opportunity to own the classic US guitars. Import and export restrictions at the time made them prohibitively expensive – and in any case they were in short supply. As a result, many turned to cheaper European names such as Framus and Hofner.

The Hofner "Violin Bass" (model 500/1) is uniquely associated with one man: Paul McCartney acquired his first 500/1 in 1960, during one of the band's many residencies in Hamburg. A left-hander, he chose this model so that it didn't look too strange when re-strung and played "upside down". Although a cheap guitar, McCartney nonetheless played it throughout the Beatles' career.

The model shown here with its custom-carved "scrolled" headstock actually belonged to none other than John Lennon. It was used on a number of his 1970s solo recordings.

TRAVIS BEAN TB-2000 1976

By the time the TB-2000 bass rolled off Travis Bean's California production line, co-designer Gary Kramer had already fled to the East Coast, setting up a rival operation in New Jersey. Like other Travis Bean and Kramer models of period, the TB-2000 pioneered the radical idea of using an aluminium neck. However, unlike their six string equivalents – for which this unusual approach to construction seemed to provide, arguably, only a marginal benefit – the aluminium neck worked well on a bass instrument, producing a "hard" consistent tone well-suited to rock playing.

Like other "Beans", the quality of craftsmanship was exemplary, and featured a "through neck" construction. This meant that the full extent of the strings – machine heads, nut, pickups and bridge – were all mounted on a single aluminium block.

Although the "wings" carved from Hawaiian koa gave the TB-2000 a traditionally wooden look, the cold feel of the metal neck proved to be unpopular with musicians, and only just over a thousand TB-2000s were originally built.

Travis Beans and (to a lesser extent) early Kramers now enjoy something of a cult following, making them increasingly attractive to collectors.

KISS PUNISHER 1998

Presenting themselves to the world as a bunch of wild, face-painted rock demons, Kiss are the closest the US ever got to Glam Rock. With a huge, fanatical fanbase, the KISS logo has officially sanctioned numerous products from condoms to NASCAR motor racing. Founder member Gene Simmons (or Chaim Witz, as his mother named him) is himself an enterprising, one-man industry, his extra-curricular activities covering – among many others – acting, lecturing, writing, book and video publishing and guitar design.

The Punisher bass has been produced in limited quantities by a number of different manufacturers. This one-off – originally owned and played by Simmons – was hand-painted by the artist Steve Kaufman, and depicts images from the band's albums.

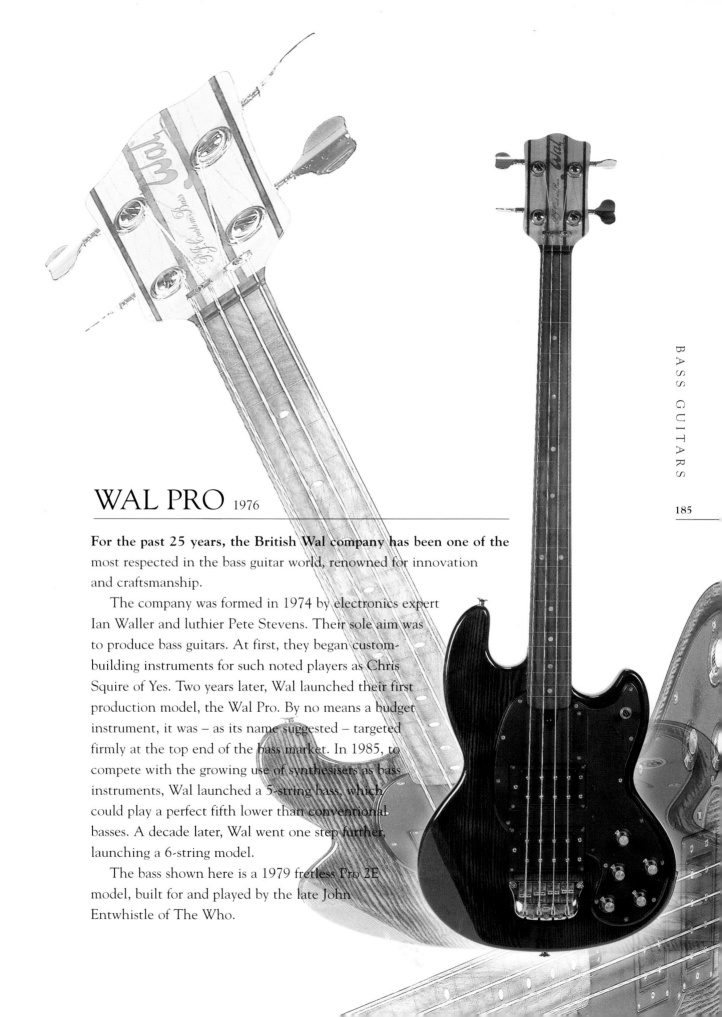

WAL PRO 1976

For the past 25 years, the British Wal company has been one of the most respected in the bass guitar world, renowned for innovation and craftsmanship.

The company was formed in 1974 by electronics expert Ian Waller and luthier Pete Stevens. Their sole aim was to produce bass guitars. At first, they began custom-building instruments for such noted players as Chris Squire of Yes. Two years later, Wal launched their first production model, the Wal Pro. By no means a budget instrument, it was – as its name suggested – targeted firmly at the top end of the bass market. In 1985, to compete with the growing use of synthesisers as bass instruments, Wal launched a 5-string bass, which could play a perfect fifth lower than conventional basses. A decade later, Wal went one step further, launching a 6-string model.

The bass shown here is a 1979 fretless Pro 2E model, built for and played by the late John Entwhistle of The Who.

AMPEG DAN ARMSTRONG 1969

The Ampeg company is rather better known for its amplification systems than its guitars. In 1969, the New Jersey company teamed up with designer Dan Armstrong to produce this unique "see-through" instrument. Made of clear plastic called Lucite, it was an attempt to produce a greater degree of sustain. Unusually for a bass guitar, the fingerboard features 24 easily accessible frets, giving a range of two octaves on each string.

The Dan Armstrong bass – and its equivalent 6-string guitar – remained in production for only two years. Even though they were highly rated by some musicians, most of the instruments were sold on the basis of their undeniably stunning visual appeal

STEINBERGER "HEADLESS" BASS 1982

As we have seen consistently throughout the gradually evolving story of the guitar over the past fifty years, when innovation is too radical, players are scared off. One instrument that – to some degree, at least – bucks this theory is the 1982 Steinberger "headless" bass guitar. This was almost a complete overhaul of the way a bass guitar should look and be constructed.

The basic premise of Ned Steinberger's design was not particularly new, but his solution was unique. He reasoned that the most important part of the bass was the neck, and that the headstock was likely to cause unwanted alterations in sound. So he got rid of it altogether! Believing also that denser materials would produce greater clarity and sustain, he chose to make his instrument almost entirely from a moulded epoxy resin called Graphite. It was claimed to have twice the density and ten times the strength of mahogany.

The resulting instrument produced a tone of startling clarity, and almost completely eliminated "wolfs" – notes whose frequencies react with those of the instrument to produce a "dead" sound.

For a period in the mid-1980s, every "hip" bass guitarist wanted to be seen playing the Steinberger. As the shape inevitably fell from fashion, Steinberger produced models with more conventionally crafted bodies.

INDEX

Guitars in **bold** are pictured

PICTURE CREDITS

The publishers would like to thank the following sources for their kind permission
to reproduce the pictures in this book:

AKG London: Erik Bohr: 151

Backbeat UK/Outline Press Ltd.: 22, 30-31, 49, 94, 138-139, 159, 178-179, 183, 187

© Christie's Images Ltd (2003): 19, 25, 32, 41, 42, 45, 46, 47, 56, 58, 70-71, 92, 116, 132, 169,
176-177, 181, 182, 184

Lebrecht Collection: Private Collection: 2, 5, 10-11, 15, 16, 17, 18, 21, 23, 24, 26, 28, 29, 32, 34-35,
36, 38-39, 50-51, 52-53, 54-55, 57, 60-61, 62-63, 64-65, 67, 68, 77, 79, 80-81, 82-83, 85, 89, 90-91, 95,
96-97, 103, 104, 105, 108, 109, 110-111, 113, 114, 120-121, 122, 123, 124-125, 128, 129, 133, 136-137,
140, 141, 142-143, 144-145,146, 147, 149, 150, 152-153, 155, 162, 163, 168, 170, 171, 180,
186; / Chris Stock: 14; /TL: 12, 13br, 13tl

Redferns: Geoff Dann: 73, 74, 76, 84, 86-87, 88, 93, 98, 99, 101, 102, 106-107, 112, 117, 118, 119,
126-127, 166, 185; / Richard Ecclestone: 37, 44, 48, 78, 130-131, 135, 148, 154, 156-57,
158; /Outline Press: 69, 75, 134, 160-161, 164, 165, 167

Roland UK Ltd.: 172, 173

Sotheby's Picture Library: 72

Stick Enterprises Inc.: 174

Terry Burrows: 115

Every effort has been made to acknowledge correctly and contact the source and/or copyright holder of
each picture, and Carlton Books Limited apologises for any unintentional errors, or omissions, which will
be corrected in future editions of this book.